MW00880233

Arletta Allen

DEFY THE ODDS
Making the Transition from Trauma to Triumph

DEFY THE ODDS
Making the Transition from Trauma to Triumph

ARLETTA ALLEN

DEFY THE ODDS
Making the Transition from Trauma to Triumph

Copyright © 2023 by Arletta Allen

wwwarlettaallen.com

Paperback ISBN: 978-1-387-38025-1

"You may not control all the events that happen to you, but you can decide not to be reduced by them."

~ Maya Angelou

DEDICATION

I dedicate this book to God,
who made the seemingly impossible, possible.

TABLE OF CONTENTS

Foreword………………………………………………….. 17

A Welcome Note to You:
Taking Off the Mask…………………………………….. 19

Chapter 1:
As You Think, So You Are………………………….…… 27

Chapter 2:
Let Go of the Past………………………………...…….. 45

Chapter 3:
Re-Define Your Vision………………………………….. 61

Chapter 4:
Step Out in Purpose…………………………….…….… 77

Chapter 5:
Rekindle Your Faith…………………………...……… 101

Chapter 6:
The Power of Forgiveness…………………….……..… 119

Chapter 7:
Reclaim Your Authentic Self………………….…..…… 133

Chapter 8:
Invest in Yourself……………………………………….. 149

Chapter 9:
Reach for Your Goals………………………………...… 163

Chapter 10:
Adopt an Attitude of Gratitude………………………….. 177

Chapter 11:
Celebrate Your Successes………………………..……… 191

A Farewell Note to You:
Wearing a New Mask………………………………………….... 203

About the Author……………………………………………..… 207

Foreword
by Keziah Love

Today, as I write this foreword to Arletta's captivating memoir, I share who she is, and all that God designed her to be. *Defying The Odds* truly speaks to Arletta's entire journey, and all that it took for her to get to where she is today. Suffice it to say that God is definitely not through with her yet. There are many real-life experiences she had to pass through as a Black woman, including betrayal, failed relationships, naysayers, racial prejudice, hatred, domestic violence, mental health, and so much more.

Arletta's life, as she relates it in this remarkable book, is authentic. It is raw. It is unfiltered. She has lived and is still living, her life above toxic narratives, while courageously defying the odds. She has had to be uncommonly strong amidst daunting setbacks, shortcomings, obstacles, defeat, persecution, and lies. Yet, she remains standing!

As you read and proceed on this journey with Arletta, allow yourself to feel, to wonder, to laugh, to cry, and to just be. There is so much that she unpacks, and I think it is just beautiful that you have allowed yourself to gain access to all that she shares from the depth of her soul. As you read her story, you will realize that God is bigger than her journey, and *your* own journey, for that matter. More importantly, you will feel yourself becoming empowered to never give up but to keep going, no matter what gets in your way.

To Arletta, herself, I have these heartfelt words to say:

Despite what was, this is your now;
No longer in chains, no longer bound.

The trials of life came to make you stronger.
Hold your head high up, because you are a survivor;
You are a conqueror.

You analyzed every situation, and compromised your own salvation;
Just to feel the voids of desolation.
You struggled to break the chains of rejection.
You couldn't handle being pushed away;
So you did all you could just to be accepted.
This caused fear to be injected into you;
And rejection became your infection.
You craved acceptance, just to avoid being neglected;
Only to find yourself manipulated.
Yet, you felt obligated to do what you had to do;
Just to feel appreciated.

You couldn't stand being rebuked and hated correction.
You loved being who you were;
But, deep down inside;
You needed a new direction;
To break free of bondage;
And the chain of rejection.

Arletta, no longer do you have to fake it to make it.
No longer do you have to wear a mask;
Or put on a façade.
You may have been rejected by man;
Ridiculed, talked about, lied upon.
But, you were always accepted by God.
You are a woman;
A woman who Defied the Odds.

Keziah Love
Fond du lac, Wisconsin
United States of America
November 2022

A Welcome Note to You
Taking off the Mask

"Very often, "what happened" takes years to reveal itself. It takes courage to confront our actions, peel back the layers of trauma in our lives, and expose the raw truth of our past. But this is where healing begins."

- Oprah Winfrey

Dear Co-Passenger on The Train of Trauma,

I became tired. I became tired of pretending to myself, and to others. I became tired of trying to meet the expectations of others. I became tired of wondering if anyone actually knew the real me. It finally occurred to me that I had wasted my greatest asset; *time*. I wore different masks to appease those around me. That meant having to conform to their belief patterns just to align their emotional and physical body language with mine. Yet, the futile outcome of all that effort was that, as soon as I began to conform to the beliefs of others around me, all I succeeded in doing was fashioning a new and inauthentic identity for myself. I would remain trapped in this new identity for many years to come. Those were years of my life that were gone forever, never to be regained in my lifetime.

I welcome you to the pages of one of the most remarkable reading journeys you will take in your own lifetime. You and I, as you read these words, are standing together on the train platform of an Amtrak station. We have a special train to take. That train is called the *'Train of Trauma,'* and we are about to embark on the journey from *Trauma To Triumph.* Standing on that station platform, and as I flip through the pages of *"WhoO Influenced You? - Three Relationships that Transformed my Life,"* a gratitude anthology I co-authored with two others, I lift up my eyes to take a closer look at you. I can see that you are wearing a mask. I recognize that mask.

First, when thinking of what a mask is, what do you first imagine? A mask is an object normally worn on the face, typically for *protection, disguise, performance,* or *entertainment.* Masks have been used since medieval times for both ceremonial and practical purposes, as well as in performing arts and for entertainment, and they are usually worn on the face. Masks are not worn for a long time. That is because masks are suffocating. They are uncomfortable. Psychologically, masks can cause you to feel *oppressed, suppressed,* and *depressed.* When masks are worn for longer than expected they can easily evoke feelings of being trapped.

I recognize the mask on your face. I also know that you have worn it for far too long. I should know. I wore that same mask for many more years than I care to remember. It is the mask I wore for so many years, trying so hard to cover up who I truly was. Fortunately, I eventually discovered the stark truth behind why I wore a mask all those years. I finally discovered the truth behind why I chose to mask my true person, and what I authentically stood for, and represented. This was much deeper than a desire to compel others to like me and accept me. I had created a false version of myself; one that I felt comfortable enough to allow others to see, possibly because that was also what I genuinely desired to be. In other words, I had subconsciously created the perfect image that appealed to my own vanity. Any attempt to conceal my real *self* from others can only mean that I was ashamed of my real *self,* and my own truth. I was engaging in a futile attempt to distract others from the truth about me and to cover the deep wound of shame.

Shame is a feeling I know only too well. It is a feeling of embarrassment and humiliation that arises out of the perception of having done something *dishonorable, immoral,* or *improper.* It is also a very painful emotion that hides profound distress. Naturally, when people experience shame, they do all in their power to hide the source of that shame. The terrible thing about shame is that it can make you believe that you are fundamentally flawed in some way. That is why, in many respects, shame is a disability. In my case, I had so internalized my shame that it ultimately resulted in an unfairly harsh evaluation of myself as a person. This ultimately led me to believe that I was a bad and worthless person, who had little or no value. I felt shame for being dirt poor. I felt ashamed for wearing hand-me-down clothes and shoes. I felt righteous shame for living a life on welfare, food stamps, and housing programs. I felt infernal shame for being a prostitute as a teenager. Mine was a rollercoaster of *shame and guilt,* and *guilt and shame.* Later, I would feel serially ashamed for being a teenage mom, a high school dropout, an earner of minimum wage, and a woman who made the poorest possible choices in men; choices that inevitably led to a series of failed marriages. Overall, I felt shame for being a total misfit.

I wore my mask admirably well. During the COVID-19 pandemic, we were counseled to wear our masks to properly cover our mouths and noses. I wore my *mask of redemption* properly, in such a way that others could only see those parts of me that I believed made me appear to be someone of worth. My human soul was hemorrhaging, so my mask not only covered but also bandaged the parts of me that bled the most. Maya Angelou, the poet, and civil rights activist, once wrote, *"There is no greater agony than bearing an untold story on the*

21

inside of you." She was right, for that has been the truth, and nothing but the absolute truth, of my own journey. For me, the burden of wearing a mask began as an adolescent. The peer pressure I was subjected to while growing up as a young girl in Fond du lac, Wisconsin, was simply beyond imagination. In truth, I was always taught to be myself and to do what made me happy. Yet, while living in Fond du lac, it took a tremendous amount of courage to break free of the need to conform to what was considered the norm. In all honesty, there is no pain more excruciating than a feeling, or being seen, as an outsider. The need to *'fit in'* became even more compelling for my impressionable mind as a child. Because of the peer pressure, I simply did all I had to do to fit in. The need to conform led me to succumb to the pressure of becoming what everyone else thought I ought to be.

Naturally, I believed that if I became more like my peers, they would become more accepting of me. Yet, I seemed to be the exact opposite of the *'golden girl image'* those others portrayed. Most certainly, *the black girl; the fat girl; the nerdy girl; the rejected girl,* were what my peers undeniably were not. My hair was tangled, coily, coarse, thick, and altogether unmanageable at times. It seemed that I was everything they were not. This led me to believe there was something terribly wrong with me. I attempted to fit into what was seen to be socially acceptable, in the process I remained compliant with the norms they dictated, rather than resting comfortably in my authentic self. That pressure to conform left me feeling inadequate and inconsistent. Worse, I never felt I measured up to their expectations. I ended up in a vicious cycle, wasting time and energy trying to figure out just what it would take for me to be accepted by those who didn't look like me, and who appeared to be all I aspired to be.

Yet, no one just wakes up on a beautiful morning and decides to wear a mask. The need to wear a mask is usually rooted in what I have chosen to call *The Inner Scream.* Indeed, there is a deep, inner part of you that screams your inadequacies, and your perceived flaws and your natural reaction is to seek and create a balm that will soothe that pain. I wore my mask to cover up the pain of my traumatic past.

That is why this train journey, as represented by the book you hold in your hands, is titled, "DEFYING THE ODDS – *Making the Transition from Trauma to Triumph."* My trauma was a combination of the pain of being compelled to conform, heartbreak, betrayal, abandonment, labels, and so much more than the average mind can cope with. I employed the simplest tool to cover my pain. I wore a smile. It was a fake smile. It is famously said that practice makes perfect. I practiced my fake smile so consistently that, soon my mask became second nature to me.

After a while, wearing the mask became a burden all its own. Putting on the mask before stepping outside gradually became too arduous to sustain. However, removing the mask was an unattractive option, since, to remove the mask, I would have to admit that I had problems. Admitting this would expose my wounds, scars, and flaws to the scrutiny of prying and judgmental eyes. That agony would have been too painful to bear, so I felt compelled to seek an alternative path to the avoidance of exposure and the pain of rejection. The only recourse was to prove that I had capabilities. So, I became an overachiever.

Today, I wear the more authentic mask of an uncommonly accomplished woman. I succeeded in completing 14 years in the financial industry as a bank teller. I graduated with an associate degree in leadership development. I obtained certifications in healthcare leadership, organizational leadership, principles of leadership, and human resource management. I graduated summa cum laude with a bachelor's degree in communication, with a minor in business. I became the first person in my immediate family to earn a college degree. I was the first person in my family to own my home. I became the first black woman to serve as a local government official in the history of the city of fond du lac, Wisconsin. I was featured on the cover of *Inspire Magazine,* a woman-centered publication. I have successfully raised four sons as a single mother. I am the founder of a non-profit, *Peculiar Princess Project, Inc.,* through which I give little girls of color the tools they need to build their self-esteem, self-value, and self-worth. I have been an ordained church minister since 2003. I opened the first black-owned restaurant in Fond du Lac, called *A Family Affair Soulfood Kitchen.* I have won national awards for self-sufficiency through the *National Community Action Partnership of America.* I have even graced the stage for TEDx which helps you share ideas with communities around the world. My *TEDx* speech is titled: *"Creating the Awe in Your Authenticity"* and can be viewed on *YouTube.*

Even with the most modest attempt at acknowledgment, this is not a mean narrative for the awkward and bumbling girl who lacked any confidence in herself many years ago. Admittedly, all these accomplishments should count as nothing short of success, but with a sense of profound gratitude, I admit that my greatest success isn't any of these accomplishments. My greatest success has been the development of the courage to strive to become my true and authentic self. My purpose in writing this book is to encourage you to do as I have done and to seek to become nothing but your true, authentic, and unapologetic self. I welcome you to the pages of a book written to encourage you to totally embrace yourself. It is only when you finally and totally embrace yourself that you will experience the true freedom that will allow you to thrive as a worthy person, and to flourish as your best self. This book will teach you how to embrace both your vulnerability, and your past, such that you will become able to showcase your *real person* in all your authenticity, and in all your true worthiness. This will empower you to defy the odds in your life.

Here, give me your hand as we both step from the station platform to board the *Train of Trauma.* I can't wait to tell you my story. It is a story of sadness, yet it is also a story of joy. This will be the train ride of your life. The beauty of the ride is that, at the end of it, you will discard your old mask, and put on a new one; a mask that will reveal both your new-found triumph and your authenticity. Let the ride begin.

Arletta Allen
Arlington, Texas
United States of America
November 2022

Chapter 1
As You Think, So You Are

"All we achieve and all that we fail to achieve
is the direct result of our own thoughts."

- James Allen And Marc Allen

In 1904, a little-known Englishman named James Allen wrote a small book called *As a Man Thinketh*. A hundred years later, this book has become a self-empowerment classic of all time. Indeed, it is a very powerful piece of literature. Author and publisher, Marc Allen, would later update the timeless literary gem, polishing the original author's message to highlight the universal principles expressed as great and eternal truths that simply and easily remind us that personal power lies within the mind and that once awakened, there are simply no limits to what one can imagine and then achieve, with the sheer power of thought. I go further to state that our thoughts bear key relationships to our personal character, life circumstances, physical health, life purpose, achievement, and personal serenity. Indeed, all we achieve, and all that we fail to achieve, is the direct result of our own thoughts. We are truly masters of our individual destinies.

As You Think

Even before I read this classic, I had always entertained the deep understanding that you are as great as you think you are. Despite my earlier handicaps and obstacles, I have managed to accomplish well beyond my expectations. I can only attribute that outcome to the fact that I sincerely believed I could accomplish the seemingly extraordinary feat. I spent years struggling with self-esteem. I struggled to believe that I was worthy of anything, or even worth anything, for that singular matter. My father was the one person I yearned to look up to for validation. When, as was the totally unfortunate case, he withheld that rather vital validation, and rather went ahead to decimate what little self-esteem I managed to possess, it was only natural for me to believe all the withering and scathing words he said to me, and about me. In other words, I took his words to be my *truth*. I allowed his unedifying characterizations of me to both define who I was, and who I thought I was.

Words are extremely powerful agents. Allow me to rephrase that sentence, as it fails to express that truth as succinctly as it deserves to be expressed. Words are the most potent force on Earth. I will explain. To start with, the enormous power contained in words is perfectly enunciated in the first words of John, in the Book of life, *'In the beginning was the Word, and the Word was with God, and the Word was God.'* Believe it or not, words are patently responsible for both the devastating effects of curses and the edifying gloriousness of prayer. That is why it is always better to emphasize nothing but the positive in any realm of one's affairs. Actually, and in sacrosanct fact, the key to proper progress in life, and ultimately, sustainable success, lies, wittingly or unwittingly, in the proper deployment of words to our subconscious mind. The subconscious mind is the hidden part of our mind, and it is extremely susceptible to the power of words. Every thought and experience we have ever had, and every word we have ever heard, all become indelibly imprinted in our subconscious mind. Inevitably, each one of us is a mere reflection of the thoughts stored in our subconscious. Incredibly, the greatest fact about the subconscious mind is that, although it possesses

28

such humongous power, it is unable to distinguish between truth and falsehood. Since it is such an irrepressible reservoir of all the influences we have had from childhood, the words we speak to our children assume an importance that simply cannot be trifled with. Countless parents have altered their child's destiny through the unguarded utterance of negative and unedifying words. Those words were automatically accepted as true by the child's subconscious, throwing her self-image into the realm of the extremely low, and psychologically incapacitating her for a significant part of her lifetime. That was my story.

I would often marvel at my father's irrational behavior towards me, and wonder just what was so wrong with me that I had to suffer so much rejection at his hands. Going down the lane of painful memory, I recall a particularly poignant day. I had arrived home from school, brimming with excitement at the prospect of sharing a new game I had learned at school with my father. Announcing myself with typical juvenile enthusiasm, I promptly jumped onto his lap and began to demonstrate the game. There was an imagined apple in my hand, and my father had to pretend to bite the apple to its core. Initially, he seemed sufficiently inclined to share in the spirit of the game, at least until I played my own part in it. What he didn't know was that as soon as he pretended to bite the apple, I was required to lightly smack the sides of his face with my small, six-year-old hands. I did just that, and all hell broke loose. My father gruffly pushed me backward, and I landed on the floor. Next, he picked me up by one ankle, and with his belt, visited me with such aggressive lashing that it became sheer agony to even attempt to sit because of the welts I suffered on my legs and backside. I distinctly recall dangling upside down, thinking with horror that he was going to drop me on my head. My horror was all but confirmed, as a few moments later, totally worn out from tussling with me, in my desperate attempt to wriggle myself out of his grasp, he actually dropped me on my head. That night, I cried myself to sleep. All I had wanted was for my father to experience the same joy I had felt in school when I shared that game with my peers. Instead, what I got was a beating for all my trouble. In retrospect, I can't even begin to fathom why I had thought my idea was a good one, to begin with. Certainly, I knew my father was a totally humorless, distant, and gruff man who did not break any attempt at frivolity and playfulness. To this day, I remain baffled at why I even bothered to expose myself to the risk of incurring his displeasure. That traumatic incident taught me that my father was not my friend, and from that moment, I learned the rather bitter lesson never to seek to connect with him on an emotional level ever again. As you think, so you are. My thoughts toward my father would change forever. Yet, that was merely the beginning of an odyssey of a poisoned thought pattern that was conceived in my mind even before I ever addressed my relationship with my father as an adolescent. One thing is, however, clear. I grew up with a dislocated thought pattern that threw me into the realm of unworthiness and self-deprecation.

The Power of Your Thoughts

Buddha, the founder of Buddhism, once said, "*The mind is everything. What you think you become.*" He was right. I believe that your thoughts are ultimately responsible for how you feel. Your feelings come from your thinking. Yet, our thoughts do not operate alone. They are closely interconnected with our emotions. Thoughts and emotions are intricately related and can be experienced together, although they are distinct. Our thoughts are mental cognitions. They are our ideas, opinions, and beliefs about ourselves and the world around us. They also incorporate the perspectives we bring to any situation or experience that can color our point of view, for better, worse, or neutral. An example of a long-lived thought is an *attitude*. That means an attitude can develop as thoughts are repeated over and over, and are reinforced. Even though our thoughts are shaped by our life experiences, they are generally under conscious control. In other words, if you are aware of your thoughts and attitudes, you can choose to change them.

Emotions, on the other hand, might be usefully seen as the flow and experience of feelings, for example, joy, sadness, anger, or fear. Our emotions can be triggered by something external, for instance, seeing a friend suffer, or watching a movie. They can also be triggered by something internal, such as a traumatic memory. Ultimately, thoughts and emotions have a profound effect on one another. My personal experience is instructive. As might be expected, I sometimes spend time dwelling on my past. At such times, if I sit for too long, thinking of my past trauma, the room, even in daylight, suddenly becomes dark and gloomy. The surprising thing is that this might even have been a day in which I had previously found myself in very high spirits. But now, having indulged my inner environment in a series of dismal thoughts about my past, I had inadvertently sunk into what I can now lucidly characterize as my *dark state of the mind.* In that pernicious state, my thoughts constantly bombard me with my past failures, and my profound feelings of inadequacy. The result is that my inner self screams, *"You are not enough!"* Then, I would descend into a vicious cycle of sorts and would find myself acting in perfect accord with that inner thought pattern. What had happened was really quite simple. I had ceded my power to my thoughts by reinforcing them, and worse, I had now placed them on *auto-pilot* mode.

Unfortunately, I seemed incapable of appreciating that whatever I gave consistent and greater thought to was what would manifest in my life. Gradually, however, with the benefit of self-observation, I gradually grew into the wisdom that my thoughts are actually my greatest assets. My thoughts possessed the enormous power to take me high or to bring me low. I will be the first person to admit that I think a lot. In fact, I probably qualify to be called an *overthinker.*

These days, my thinking binge has taken me into a fascinating realm. *Is it possible to deploy the power of your thoughts to financial gain?* Recently, I have had to devote some thought to my finances. My financial stability has been somewhat rocked by my current circumstances. I am divorced and single. I am relocating from one state to another. Significantly, I am in the rather arduous process of restructuring my business model. In all these, I have no one to depend on, except God and myself. How will these all work out? I haven't a clue what's on the other side of the horizon, yet I am of absolute certainty that, somehow, I will see myself through my current challenges.

I seem to be in a state of consciousness that speaks nothing but the language of success to my soul. In fact, every time I imagine failure, I find myself asking God to forgive me for my thoughts of self-deprecation and ingratitude. I immediately arrest such thoughts and reject what I instantly recognize to be the enemy of my soul intent on planting the seed of doubt and discord in my mind. I am reminded that I am the daughter of the King. I am reminded that, just as God has rescued me from myself in the past, this current situation will be no different. Besides, I have the eternal promise that God remains the same today, yesterday, and forevermore. I choose to stand firmly on that promise. I now acknowledge that there is enormous power in my thoughts and even greater power in my prayers. God will uphold His promises towards me, for I am not only a great success by His might, but a masterpiece because I am a piece of the master.

> *I am a mortal image of His Immortality.*
> *I am a finite portion of His Infinity.*
> *I am eternal through His Eternity.*
> *I am mighty by His Might.*
> *I am a masterpiece;*
> *Because I am a piece of the Master.*
>
> *- Arletta Allen*

Value the Quality of Your Life

The quality of your thoughts determines your ability to enjoy your life. I hasten to admit that, as I write, my thoughts at this current stage of my life are not of a quality that I am particularly proud of. Indeed, at this critical and significant stage of my life, I sincerely believe I could entertain thoughts that are more edifying. Yet, I am truly loath to label my thoughts, especially at such a critical intersection in my life journey. I am transitioning to a new place, and a new location, and I am filled with trepidation. I am fearful of the unknown. I am afraid because of all the potential *what-ifs.*

What if I can't really afford this relocation?

What if I become acutely lonely in my new location and neighborhood?

What if my mother needs me, and I am inaccessible?

What if my sons have an urgent need for my presence?

What if my career doesn't take off on the trajectory that I'm praying for?

What if, what if, what if...

Everyone has moments where they worry about the *what-ifs*. They are actually a necessary part of life and assist us in the decision-making process. They can also motivate us to make better choices. Yet, they can become overwhelming. The *what-if* questions are bound to come up at certain points in our life journey, especially during major life decisions. They help us weigh the *pros* and *cons*, evaluate all angles of the decision, and even help us to determine if these are actually decisions we are ready to make. It is when these questions distort our thought process so much that we are robbed of our peace of mind that we have a problem. Questioning every possible event, outcome, or result can only lead us to doubt our abilities.

The worst part is that, in most cases, we do not even have a realistic way to answer these *what-if* questions. Since we don't have an answer, we predict what will happen or make up possible scenarios in our minds. The cycle can easily spin out of control. Our mind manufactures the *what-if* questions. We have no adequate answers to the questions. So, we make up answers. The answers cause us even greater anxiety, which causes more questions, and the cycle continues. How do we put a stop to this? In my own case, something remarkable happened. I remembered that the quality of my thoughts determines how much peace I have in my life, and by extension, the quality of my life. I realized I could neutralize my negative *what-if* questions with positive *what-if* questions.

What if God's promises are true?

What if God could give me peace?

What if God really is faithful?

What if I could trust God for everything?

What if God really does love me unconditionally?

What if my fear of the unknown could focus instead on the known?

Ultimately, my thoughts are mine, whether they are of low, excellent, good or bad quality. I believe it is important that I become more mindful of my thoughts so that those *what-ifs* of doubt and fear do not become my reality. At this stage of my life, the quality of my life has assumed truly great significance. This is because, having been subjected to so much suffering in my life, I feel under a certain obligation to situate myself at a better and more enjoyable place in life.

I struggled so hard just to make ends meet. I watched my parents struggle even harder to make ends meet. I lived in a homeless shelter, while my mother struggled to provide better shelter. To this day, these harrowing memories remain a recurring nightmare for me. I recall those times when my mother had to wearily trudge over to the corner store in the neighborhood to get a couple of cans of baked beans and a package of hot dogs to feed her six children on credit until she could get her food stamps to pay back her debt. We had no money because my father was living a double life, and would often leave my mother for weeks at a time to be with his other family on the hill, as my mom would say. In retrospect, my father's eventual departure from our lives was probably a matter of total indifference to my mother. Certainly, my observation was that his final exit brought long-desired peace of mind to her. She sang more often after he left us. She sewed more, and she became more engaged with us.

My mother was a guru at creating something out of nothing. She transformed the fare of baked beans and hot dogs into a phenomenal meal of survival for my siblings and me. When I got older and had my four sons to feed, I prepared this meal for them purely out of enjoyment, and not out of a despairing state of indigence. I merely used the meal to celebrate a phase in my life in which my mother turned our *lime into lemonade.* As a young mother, I had managed to refine the quality of my thoughts to the point where I could create a life for my sons that saw no need to be ashamed of the classic poor man's meal of baked beans and hot dogs. Rather, I embraced it. I have no idea why I am so emphatic about using this story to illustrate the essence of *quality of life,* one way or the other, but that is what occurs to me as I think of a life in which, although I was never served steak, my mother still managed to prepare and present every meal in such a manner that made me believe that I actually lacked for nothing as a child.

Alter Your Self-Image

Robert Kiyosaki once wrote, *"It's not what you say out of your mouth that determines your life, it's what you whisper to yourself that has the most power!"* This businessman and the author are right. Your self-image is, in its most basic form, an internalized mental picture or idea you have of yourself. It is how you think and feels about yourself based on your appearance and performance, and those relationships that consistently impact your outlook on life, as well as your level of happiness and fulfillment.

How do I look?

How am I doing?

How important am I?

These are all examples of the internalized mental picture or idea you create of yourself, which serves to build the foundation of your self-image. Permit me to break it down even further. Your self-image is the impression you have of yourself that forms a collective representation of your assets and liabilities. In other words, your self-image is how you see yourself based on your strengths and weaknesses. These assets and liabilities are often evident through the labels you ascribe to yourself, describing your qualities and characteristics. For instance, you might say, *I am intelligent... therefore I can... I am a loser... therefore I believe I can't... I am outgoing... therefore I am able to... I am shy... therefore I am unable to...*

These are merely some of the examples of the many labels you potentially give yourself, and the inevitable conclusions you may arrive at. It is these conclusions you reach about yourself that either form the foundations of a healthy self-image or an unhealthy self-image. Moreover, these labels form the foundation of your belief system. Your self-image is not something that is based on reality. In actuality, your self-image is built upon your perception of reality, and that is influenced by how you believe you are viewed by other people. Your self-image is something that gradually develops over a lifetime of experience, through learning and societal influence. It is, however, something that is constantly evolving over time as you gain more life experience, as you think and reflect, as you learn, and as you interact with other people. A person with an unhealthy self-image tends to consistently focus on flaws and limitations. In fact, they persistently criticize themselves and tend to judge most of their decisions and actions. *What was I thinking? That was such a stupid decision. I can't believe I just did that.*

This constant critical judgment tends to distort their imperfections, making them larger than life. In fact, everything on the negative side tends to be exaggerated and blown out of proportion. This often happens because they are heavily influenced by other people's opinions of them to their own detriment. In fact, these people's lives are very much defined by societal standards, norms, and expectations. As a result, they are consistently comparing themselves to others and trying to live up to other people's expectations. When they notice that they just don't measure up to such, almost always, unrealistic expectations, their emotions go into a tailspin to trigger doubt, pessimism, and insecurity. Whenever a person builds their self-image upon external factors, there will always be drawbacks. People's opinions change and societal expectations constantly shift. When these opinions and expectations are weighed in our favor, this leads to a positive outlook and more fulfillment. However, when they flip and become unfavorable or unhelpful in respect to the outcomes we would like to achieve, this causes upheaval in us by sending our emotions into a tailspin because, suddenly, the perfect mental picture we had of ourselves has been shattered, and we are shattered.

A healthy self-image, on the other hand, is primarily based on an individual's personal feelings and perspectives. An individual is no longer influenced by other people's opinions of them, or by societal expectations. Instead, they make up their own minds about the internalized mental picture they have of themselves. As a result, these people often have a more optimistic outlook on life and thereby more confidence in themselves and in their own abilities. Not unnaturally, that is because they feel a greater sense of control over themselves, and over their life. People with healthy self-images do not deny that they have flaws. In fact, they are realistic about those flaws, and clearly understand and accept the fact that they have their personal shortcomings. However, there is no critical judgment here. They acknowledge who they are, and how they are at this material moment and do the best they can with what they have. A healthy self-image is, naturally, built upon a high level of self-worth. Both of them work together to help shape a healthy personality, which effectively builds the foundations of an empowered life.

In order to change your self-image from negative to positive, it is of paramount importance to have a clear understanding of who you really are. There have been too many occasions when I looked in the mirror, and didn't like what I saw. This was particularly true when I was pregnant with my sons. I never could quite reconcile myself to the changes to a body that never returned to its original form. Unfortunately, those changes to my body shape robbed me of my ability to continue to see myself as an attractive and desirable woman. In fact, after I had my first son, I fell into a deep depression, a state which I believe is clinically referred to as a postpartum depression. Additionally, I was no longer able to see myself as a good mother. To all intents and purposes, I turned away from my son, neglecting him in the process.

As I was only sixteen at that time, I was living at home with my mother. My mother made it a point to teach me a valuable lesson. She said, *"You had this baby. You're gonna raise this baby!"* My mother wouldn't allow me to go anywhere without my infant right at my side. One day, the phone rang. This was in the day of the landlines when cell phones had not yet taken over our lives. I was changing my son's diaper on the couch. He was no more than three or four weeks old. Motherhood was an entirely novel experience for me. Abandoning the baby, I ran to answer the phone. The next thing I heard was a loud and resounding thud, followed by a high-pitched squeal. I dropped the phone and ran back into the living room. My baby had rolled off the couch, and onto the floor. I swooped in like a knight in a cape and picked my baby up. His little diaper was dangling around his leg. Apparently, I had not even secured it well enough. I recall swaddling him in his blanket, pulling him tightly to my bosom, rocking him back and forth, and sitting on the floor. I wept uncontrollably because I thought I had *'broken'* him. Shortly thereafter, my mother came in and asked, *"What is wrong with y'all? Both y'all crying."* I told my mother what had happened, and she said, *"Girl, hand me that boy. He is just fine. His limbs stretch like rubber bands at this stage. It's almost impossible to break him. Now, stop being afraid for him, because he can feel that."*

My mother was being her vintage self. She had a way of educating me on the fundamental things without making me feel stupid. I might have been a mere child mothering my child, but my mother ensured that before she released me to go out into the world, I knew perfectly well how to take care of myself and mine. Even at that, being a high school dropout ultimately caused me to view myself as dumb, slow, and unintelligent. The only way I could change the way I viewed myself was to go back to school and finish what I had started. I received my high school equivalency diploma and worked at the nearby burger joint called Tuckers, to earn sufficient money to buy diapers and baby formula for my son. As individuals, we are constantly evolving and changing according to what we see when we look in the mirror. My self-image was important to me. It controlled whether or not I had sufficient strength to rise out of bed from one day to the next. I believe I worked hard at the many stages of my life to reinvent myself, or the way I saw myself if I didn't like what I saw. I took in what I saw around me as a child, and as I grew into adulthood, I seemed to know all the changes I wanted to make about myself. Education wasn't something my family was already accomplished at, therefore my dropping out of school was totally unacceptable. I promised myself that my future would be brighter than the one my parents potentially offered me. In order to defy the odds, I knew I needed to get those degrees. I did. I have dedicated much of my life to redefining the generational baton that was handed to me. I will not stop altering my self-image and re-inventing myself until I become incapable of further change. Each day, we are gifted new mercy, and fresh grace, to renew our attempt at betterment, and with each attempt, we gain more experience. Indeed, I can always become better, even if only in my own eyes.

The Power of the "Sticky" Note

Whenever I think of sticky notes, I also think of labels. To be consistently told all that you are not, and all that you will never be, as an adolescent, is a huge amount of homework piling up for you to tackle as an adult. Sticky notes are small pieces of colorful paper, usually square, with a lightweight adhesive strip on the back, made for temporarily attaching notes to documents and other surfaces. The low-tack pressure-sensitive adhesive allows the notes to be easily attached, removed, and even re-posted elsewhere without leaving residue.

Sticky notes helped me to redefine the way I labeled myself. Close on the heels of my father's death in 2009, I found myself swimming through all possible *highs* and *lows* of grief. I was reminded of all the times I was told I was not good enough for anything worthy of commendation. Sticky notes were the tool that I used to paint my mirror a kaleidoscope of colors and to leave words that echoed at a frequency that differed vastly from the messages of deprecation and *put down* that I had consistently been subjected to through the years. I was broken, humiliated, and angry. How could my father simply and abruptly decide to leave me after just getting to know the 28-year-old adult me? We had been separated since I was only 11 years old. My father lived over 800 miles away from me. The only memories I had of him were those that haunted and traumatized me, and to put the icing on the cake of uninspiring memories of him, I was now left with images of him on a hospital bed. At the end of his life, the radiation treatments for cancer caused swelling in his throat, so he could not speak because of the tracheostomy tube that was inserted into his throat to help him breathe. I recall being at his bedside to offer him the comfort of knowing that I had forgiven him for all the pain he caused me, including those terrible wounds he had inflicted on me, which he was blissfully unaware of.

After the funeral, I came back to my isolated apartment with my boys and promptly gave in to my pent-up grief. I fell apart behind those walls. There had been no time for an appropriate closure to a lifetime of a severely fissured relationship between father and daughter. There had been no time for healing. He had simply left me in the throes of agony from an open wound. The only words that continued to ring in my consciousness, like echoes in a dank, dark cave, were those demeaning words he had hurled at me; *dirty, whore, slut, no daughter of* mine. Now, how do you go about detaching yourself from such malignant and malevolent labels that seem irrevocably affixed to the core of your soul? It was not an impossible task. But, it took a tremendous amount of work.

42

I cultivated a new habit. It was a habit that would impact my life much more significantly than I could have ever imagined. I began to write on yellow sticky notes. On those notes, I wrote out all the things I desired to be known for; *beautiful, smart, happy, funny, trustworthy, loyal, caring, kind, and strong.* At one point, there were so many sticky notes that I eventually started sticking them to the wall in my bathroom, so that the mirror could still serve its purpose, which it only barely did. The sticky notes were bright and conspicuous, and whenever I felt low in spirit or began to doubt who I was, I was certain that in the morning, and at bedtime, I was guaranteed a bright reminder on the wall close to my bed. Gradually, I started to enter into a state of rest, and of peace. I was gradually letting go of the long-ingrained belief that I was defined by the labels that were previously attached to me, and was now slowly, and ever so slowly, substituting those labels with the powerful and empowering words on my sticky notes. Those sticky notes possessed and expressed the power that gave me the ability to relabel myself into a person of beauty, worth, and esteem.

Chapter 2
Let Go of the Past

---

*"Future successes can be diminished by carrying baggage
from the past. Let go of the excess baggage."*

- Reed B. Markham

About 3,000 years ago, two monks were walking in deep
silence along the banks of a river, high up in the mountains.
The two monks were devout followers of Buddha and
had taken a vow of chastity that forbade them from ever
speaking to, or even touching a woman. Suddenly, the scream
of a woman broke the silence of the valley. In the distance, the
two monks could sight a woman who was desperately trying to
swim the river to reach her child on the other side. The poor
woman was obviously too frightened to cross the river all by
herself. One of the monks walked over to her. He picked her
up, carried her across the river, and set her down by her child,
he returned to join his friend. They resumed their walk in
silence. About two hours later, the other monk broke the
silence.

"I can't believe you spoke to that woman. I can't believe
you actually carried her across the river. I can't believe you
touched her. I can't believe you broke your vows. I put her
down two hours ago. You are the one who is still carrying her,"
his friend replied quietly, looking very calmly and
meaningfully at him. The moral of this story from this folklore
is simple. We often carry our problems, and our past,
around with us long after we should have discarded them, or
"put them down," so to speak.

Your Past is Excess Baggage

The majority of us are guilty of living in the *ugliness* of *our* yesterday instead of living in the *beauty* of *our* today. What are you still carrying around that really isn't happening anymore? What are you still hanging onto that isn't in your present moment? Are you still simmering in anger from that argument you had yesterday? Are you still in emotional agony over that broken relationship? Believe it or not, it is only when you have put down what you are still carrying around that you can have your hands, heart, and mind free to pick up the new experiences that are waiting to enrich your life today.

We all have suitcases. They are an inevitable component of our material existence. We need them to transport our clothes and sundry other times when we embark on our journeys from one place to another. Even when we are not on a trip, we need them to store those clothes that are not in season, and which do not immediately need to grace space in our closet. Like anyone else, I had suitcases. But, I had another type of suitcase. That suitcase was one that was filled to its brim with my issues. Worse, I got into the unfortunate habit of lugging that suitcase around with me, anywhere I went. Nothing is a greater burden than a suitcase full of issues. Nothing poses a greater threat to proper progress in life than the perceived obligation of lugging around a suitcase filled with issues.

There is a name for a suitcase of issues. It is called *emotional baggage.* My emotional baggage was composed, in the main, of unresolved emotional turmoil from my past. The emotional baggage from my previous relationships continued to plague me long after I ought to have consigned those relationships to the garbage can of my history. To this day, I still struggle with understanding how to move on from the chronic trauma I suffered through the years. I have been married twice. To my own detriment, I carried so much baggage from the first marriage into the second one.

To say that my first marriage was devastating would be putting the entire experience very mildly. There is no greater recipe for matrimonial disaster than bringing two wounded individuals together in a futile attempt to make one whole and complete being. Marriage is the only entity in which the mathematical summation of *one plus one* is acknowledged to be one. Unfortunately, when the actors in the union are two traumatized individuals, that equation is rendered totally invalid. It just cannot work that way in such a union.
I met my first former husband when I was only sixteen years old, and I became pregnant almost immediately. Still, in search of the security and validation that true maturity might have provided, we plunged into marriage three years later. Suffice it to say that, with little or no guidance, our major preoccupation was simply how to figure out life. I was coming from the background of *daddy issues*. He was coming from a background of *mama* and *daddy issues.* As might be expected, that shared background basically provided us a place of pain at which we could safely connect. That, at least, was something we had in common. He had spent most of his young life incarcerated.

I had spent most of my juvenile life in an identity crisis. That meant we both had bags filled with physical abuse, emotional trauma, and psychic agony, and we both lugged those bags into our marriage, and in the process of peering into each other's bags, we inevitably took solace and consolation in a mutual codependence on each other to survive, from one day to the next. He never gave himself the opportunity to address his grief and suffered on a daily basis because he refused to unpack his pain from that baggage of trauma. He allowed the trauma to eat away at him, day in, and day out. The worst was yet to come, as he would experience his deepest grief when his mother passed away at the age of forty-one. She had gone into a cardiac arrest from which she never recovered. He was shattered, and could never get over his grief. In defense, he erected a steel and impenetrable wall that was totally impervious to communication, even at the most fundamental level. It was my unfortunate lot to be married to a broken man, helplessly and inadequately trying to fix what I did not even have access to in the first place. In the circumstances, I drove myself to a state of mental exhaustion in my attempt to heal him, totally oblivious of the fact that it was not even my job to heal him in the first place. I assumed responsibility for his pain, somehow finding a way to ingeniously make that pain mine also. The end result was that, despite the fact that I had little or no room for added trauma, I went ahead to add even more trauma to my own baggage, which was already filled to excess.

If my first marriage was a nightmare, my second marriage was hell on Earth. My second husband was a *narcissistic sociopath.* A narcissistic sociopath is someone who demonstrates traits and symptoms of both narcissistic personality disorder and antisocial personality disorder. Such persons derive a somewhat savage satisfaction from manipulating, deceiving, using, and abusing others in order to get what they want. Often, they employ human charm, charisma, humor, or other deceptive disguises, to get people to like and trust them, making it harder, at least in the beginning, to detect their narcissistic and sociopathic traits.

I will attempt to explain the components of a narcissistic sociopath personality. *A narcissistic personality disorder* is characterized by a grandiose sense of self-importance, an attitude of entitlement or arrogance, and an excessive need for external validation. In other words, such persons have an inflated, grandiose, or arrogant view of themselves, and demonstrate this in how they interact with others. They are primarily driven by a need for external validation, which they might seek out in the form of praise, power, success, or attention from others. A person with an *antisocial personality disorder* is impulsive, aggressive, and has a total disregard for rules, laws, and social norms. Such a person is emotionless, detached, or cold, and is either unable or unwilling to consider the feelings or needs of other people. They tend to be driven by impulses, destructive urges, and in some instances, a desire to harm others. A *narcissistic sociopath* has both disorders and is considered one of the most dangerous and psychologically disturbed kinds of people. That is because their complete lack of empathy, or regard for the feelings or needs of other people, makes them much more likely to act out behaviors that most people would consider wrong, bad, or even outright evil. A narcissistic sociopath is not only driven by self-interest, but can also be sadistic, and derive pleasure or satisfaction from the suffering of other people, a trait that makes such an individual quite predictable and dangerous, as they may deceive, exploit, or harm someone even when there is nothing for them to gain from doing so.

My second husband was a classic narcissistic sociopath. Everything he ever did was manipulative and with absolutely negative motives and undertones. I believe that he had endured some form of severe trauma in his childhood that created baggage that he just couldn't let go of. I recall him sharing a whole lot of horror stories from his past with me. Without a doubt, those horrifying experiences eventually affected his entire view and perception of life. He had trusted and loved those closest to him. Like me, he had suffered untold trauma in a disruptive and dysfunctional household. This is not a feeble attempt to make excuses for him or the baggage he carried.

Perhaps, however, I am on a subconscious mission to justify his ill-conceived and totally misguided actions toward me. I cannot claim to be absolutely clear about my mission here, but I do distinctly recall the famous quote, *"Hurt people, hurt People."* Ultimately, our future conduct and actions are a collective result of what was planted in us by those who were responsible for laying the foundation for our personality. Therefore, my intention is not to play the *blame game,* but simply to seek genuine growth from my own experiences.

Break Free of Toxic Relationships

Breaking free from all that seemed to have broken me appeared to be a near impossibility. One of the hardest roads I have ever traveled was escaping the control, and the hold, that a relationship that was no longer serving my best interest had on me. Yet, I finally arrived at the point where I had to make the critical choice between those toxic aspects of my existence and my very survival as a whole being. If I stayed with them, I would perish from the stress and anxiety they represented in my life. On the other hand, if I left, there was the possibility that I could now have a life in which I could experience wholeness and completeness. These options stared me fully in the face as I found myself packing up everything I valued, while courageously discarding all that could only continue to weigh me down, disallowing me from blissfully surrendering to the peace I so much desired in my life.

At that critical point, I also had to clearly define what it meant to be in a toxic relationship. A toxic relationship is one that makes you feel unsupported, misunderstood, demeaned, or attacked. On a basic level, any relationship that makes you feel worse rather than better can become toxic over time. A relationship is toxic when your well-being is threatened in some way; emotionally, psychologically, and even physically. Relationships that involve physical or verbal abuse are definitely toxic. Yet, as I discovered in my own experience, there are other far more subtle signs of a toxic relationship. At different periods in my childhood, and in my marriage, I felt I was giving more than I was getting, making me feel devalued. I felt continually disrespected, and that took a toll on my self-esteem over time. Certainly, there were those times when I felt unsupported, misunderstood, and demeaned. My first husband and I, both coming from very similar backgrounds of parental dysfunction, brought out the worst in each other. In both of my marriages, but much worse with my second husband, I felt like I had to walk on eggshells around them to keep from becoming a target of their venom. In both cases, I was never my best self around them. In acting out the misplaced role of a healer, I spent so much time, and expended so much emotional energy, trying to encourage them and to cheer them up. Sadly, especially so with my second husband, I was always to blame. He would always turn things around such that his own inadequacies and faults suddenly became mine to own.

When I arrived at the vital intersection on the road that is my life journey, I had endured all of twenty-three years of being ill in spirit, suppressing my true feelings, silencing my own voice, and pretending I could safely navigate the cesspool I had grown accustomed to; the pit called marital relationships. Subconsciously unknown to me, the mere act of inhaling the toxic fumes surrounding me had begun to choke the very life force out of me. I felt overwhelmed and exhausted from the enormous amount of pressure I was subjected to, just so as to meet the needs of those to whom I had committed myself, all the while neglecting my own needs and sanity.

51

When I came to the decision that it was time to do something different, I hadn't a clue what would be required of me. I just knew that, even if it would be forcibly done, I had to set myself free from the confined and restricted condition in which I found myself. In retrospect, I was actually losing the real essence of *myself*. From a graphic point of view, my breathing had become more and more shallow as I faded into the background of my toxic situation. Realizing that my very life was under threat, I believe my ultimate saving grace was that I was sure that I did not want to die prematurely, as there was still so much more I desired, and so much more I dreamed about. I suddenly realized I had neglected the wonderful possibilities that were mine to claim if I would choose to simply let go, and surrender all to God. Yet, even that thought itself seemed to have taken me captive. I now felt like I had disappointed God by allowing my circumstances to cause me to stray away from Him. My guilt was understandable since I found myself praying less and less, reading my bible less and less, and meditating less and less on the truths of God's word.

I recall the desperation I felt at wanting to break free from my first marriage. Matters could not have been otherwise. I was constantly cheated on and abused domestically in the most horrendous manner imaginable. I was pinched, dragged, choked, slammed, and had all sorts of objects hurled at me, all to silence my cry about what was hurting so deeply within me. He would stay out at night, drinking all of his money away, totally neglecting me. Totally refusing to build our relationship, he shattered my trust in him, over and over again, as from one week to the next, he chose the bed of another woman he was not avowed to over mine. On my own part, I resolved to remain faithful to our vows, and to the virtues of the Proverbs 31 woman. The questions kept gnawing away at my mind. What happens when your best efforts appear insufficient? What happens when your partner cannot seem to silence his demons long enough to value you as the person he is supposed to be committed to? I gradually grew tired of not being enough to make him happy, not being enough as a mom, not being enough as a wife, not being enough as a provider, and not being adequate in appearance. I was taken back to my childhood, and the labels my father gave me of being never enough. Finally, it was time for me to break free.

I remember the incident, almost as if it occurred just yesterday. I was in a panic because my husband and I were due to return the vehicle we had rented as a stop-gap measure because our own vehicle was under repairs for a slight fender bend. I had gone to the bank, where I was also employed at the time, to withdraw funds, and found, to my utter dismay, that the money had been withdrawn. I was left with only $17 to my name, and four sets of eyes looking at me to be provided for. I felt a sinking feeling of devastation. I called my former husband in a panic. He admitted that he had drawn out every dime we had. Worse, he had deserted me, as he was on a Greyhound bus, traveling from Wisconsin to Florida with his newfound love, a stripper, to start a new life. Without the least attempt at a warning, the man just left me in debt, with a broken marriage, broken faith, and four devastated sons, both to raise and to offer an explanation for the sudden tsunami that had overtaken us as a family. It all felt as if someone had suddenly pulled the floor from underneath me, and I was about to plunge into a yawning abyss, deep down below the Earth. Although I knew I had to figure out where and how to draw strength to go on, that was the final straw for me.

In the final analysis, it was from my mother that I drew the strength and fortitude to carry on. I recalled my mother's struggle with my father, and decided in my heart, and in my mind, that if my mother could weather the storm, and take us to a place of safety when I was a child, then I certainly could get my own children to a place of safety too. All I had to do was model my mother's attitude. That marked my exit from my first marriage and the journey to becoming a single mother. I gathered my children together and told them that their father had moved away, and assured them they had nothing to worry about because mommy would never let them down. I prepared a quick meal of boxed macaroni, cheese, and fish sticks. I prayed over my children and watched as they rested in full confidence, knowing that I would be their source of stability. That night, I went into my bedroom, lying prostrate on the floor, holding nothing.

I cried out to God to grant me release from this marriage that was no longer a safe place for me. I filed for divorce, and I never looked back. I continued to work full-time at the bank to provide for my children and relied on resources from the National Community Action Partnership to sustain me while I struggled to make ends meet. Founded on the philosophy that every family should have an opportunity for survival and success, the Community Action Partnership is a national, 501(c)3 nonprofit membership organization that provides resources like housing, head start programs, food, and emergency shelter, if needed, in an attempt to fight family poverty in America. The resources they provide readily contributed to me becoming self-sufficient today. Anyhow, I was finally free from what was breaking me, although the responsibility of raising my children alone was such a heavy burden on my shoulders. Yet, I carried my sons until they could carry themselves. Once again, I had defied the odds. Not one of my children was ever taken from me to be placed outside of my own care.

Conduct a Proper Burial of the Past

In its classic definition, burial, also known as interment, is a method of final disposition whereby a dead body is placed into the ground as a final rite of passage. This is usually accomplished by excavating a pit or trench, placing the deceased in it, and covering it with soil. Burying the past means letting go of your worst experiences in the past, as distinct from burying the beautiful moments of your life. Nothing is more tragic in life than living in an unpleasant past, rather than living in the glorious moment. It is only when you have buried the demons of your past that you can have your heart free to accommodate the loving nature of God and enjoy His promises of abundant life. Indeed, the greatest favor you can offer yourself is to bury the past, along with the shovel with which you dug the grave. Throw that shovel into the grave of misery, and use another shovel; the shovel of renewed hope in living, to cover up the grave with soil. Then, say goodbye to the graveside of your trauma. That is how to defy the odds, and progress from trauma to triumph. In saying goodbye to the graveside of your trauma, as Noor Shirazie, Pakistani-born author and poet, wrote,

"Bury the past, along with the shovel. Don't sprint back to what's familiar in an attempt to regain your footing. You'll fall. You'll fall every time, and wonder why the hell it's become so difficult to stand up."

The very notion of burying my past seemed like the perfectly logical thing to do until it felt as if my past was burying me. The one thing I did finally admit to myself was that, since tomorrow is not guaranteed, any delay in conducting a proper burial of my past could only end up ruining my present. Yet, it was also clear to me that I was delaying putting my past to rest merely out of the misguided fear that, at least on the subconscious level, I still needed access to what was dead. This type of mindset was only delaying my blessings, and I was not making as much progress as I knew I was capable of. I held onto relationships out of fear of abandonment. As a carryover from observing my parents as a young girl, it had been ingrained in me that the best way to overcome adversity was to suppress it. Better still, the best way to acknowledge and confront trouble was simply to pretend that trouble did not exist. As I grew into adulthood, however, I began to realize that remaining in denial of past trauma, and like an ostrich burying its head in the sand, refusing to address it simply leads to explosions in other areas of your life. It was at that point that I decided to cultivate a new habit in my life. That attitude is called the *wisdom of acceptance.* The best way to disallow your past to dictate your future is to accept what once was. You are now perfectly willing to say, *"Yes, this happened, but I now choose to recognize that it is over, and learn the lesson it teaches me."*

As I have come to understand, the greatest freedom we possess as human beings is the power of choice, and in no aspect of our existence does that power seek greater expression than in the *wisdom of acceptance*, for you can choose to refuse to accept that which no longer serves your best interest, choose to acknowledge that which you can do nothing about, and seek the wisdom to accept that the past belongs in the past, and not in the present. That also means recognizing that the power that the pain of the past possessed is now dead. Anything that is dead needs, indeed, demands, to be buried. Accept that you are just a human being that is subject to human feelings and emotions. That is called *vulnerability.* Vulnerability is one of the most precious qualities anyone can possess.

Coming from a place in which I was quick to form an outer shell and barrier around myself to avoid getting hurt because I had been emotionally injured so much in the past, it is almost unbelievable how, these days, I consider vulnerability easily my greatest asset. Many of us were not taught how to express our emotions freely. For whatever reason, maybe our home situation, childhood trauma, or perhaps our parents never ever expressed their own emotions freely, we grew up stifling and bottling up our emotions. I spent my young life terrified of others not liking me.

Therefore, an aspect of me revolved around people-pleasing, hiding what I considered my faults, and trying to compensate for my perceived inadequacies. Connecting with others by accepting your vulnerability, as opposed to overcompensating and trying to get everyone to like you, will result in some of the best interactions and relationships of your life. A lot of people, especially those who spend their entire lives covering up their emotions, have a hard time knowing exactly what vulnerability is. Vulnerability is consciously choosing to not hide your emotions or desires from others. You just freely express your thoughts, feelings, desires, and opinions regardless of what others might think of you. Vulnerability is the path to true human connection. As author Robert Glover said in his book, *No More Mr. Nice Guy,* *"Humans are attracted to each other's rough edges."* You are entitled to your rough edges. Stop trying to be perfect. Expose your true self and share yourself without inhibition. Take the rejections and move on because you are who you are, and no one else.

It is hugely important to conduct a proper burial of the past. This will prevent the stench or odor of what is dead and decaying from creeping up into what is alive and thriving in your life. Getting the proper help to navigate your past will provide the much-needed closure that will prevent you from entering into a vicious cycle of trying to figure out why things didn't work out the way you had hoped or the way you had planned. Although the disappointment can be quite real, investing time and energy into your healing can open the door to a much brighter future ahead.

Refuse to Dig Up the Past

Totally horrific and offensive as it may sound, grave thieves do exist. The biggest reason why thieves rob graves is to dispose of corpses of valuables and sell them for profit. Both historically, and even in modern times, people were buried in their finest clothes and jewelry. Robbers would dig up graves to steal jewels, fine clothing, and valuables. Luckily, there is not much to recommend the pilfering of the grave to which you consigned your traumatic past. The only thing valuable about a traumatic past is the lesson you learn from the experience. That is why it will profit you nothing to go back to exhume the past from its resting place. Yet, it takes a firmly made-up mind, and tremendous willpower, not to dig up, or revisit past disappointments, devastation, and trauma that have been laid to rest. I am of the firm conviction that you can will yourself to achieve just about anything you set your mind upon. No matter how bad it hurts to deny yourself the liberty of access to something or someone that was once a priority, you can walk away, and never look back. Let the dead bury itself, while you continue on the journey of your life. In retrospect, I will have to admit that I dissipated many years of my life dwelling on things that were entirely beyond my control. That is why, with that wisdom of hindsight, it simply cannot make sense to invest time and energy into dismissing and burying those things in my life that no longer serve my best interests, only for me to retrace my steps to go and dig them back up, and relive the trauma, all over again.

The entire process is traumatic, all by itself. Every time God would answer my prayer, and deliver me from what was causing me harm, my flesh would crave, and cry out in agony for, the poison of trauma all over again. It wasn't until I actually became *tired of being tired* that I finally refused to go back to what I knew was toxic for me. I came to the conclusion that I deserved better for myself. No one else had the decision-making power to shape my future outside of myself. Circumstances may have impacted or influenced my future and caused me setbacks, but ultimately, it was my refusal to continue to accept that which no longer served my best interests that placed me on the path of triumph.

Nature abhors a vacuum. My decision to bury the past, and my refusal to dig up that past, created a vacuum that needed to be filled. My healing process started to fill that vacuum by replacing the bitterness and pain that had taken residence in my heart. Denial and refusal, unhelpful as they may be, are actually learned disciplines that must be practiced consistently in order to become relevant in one's life. They must be unlearned for one to let go of the past. There are benefits that accrue from letting go of what was, and the biggest of them all is the gift of embracing what is to come. Although I am no longer married, I have peace. I am no longer tormented by someone else's insecurities. I have become fully responsible for shaping my own future, and that is where my energy and focus now reside. I encourage you to practice the discipline of acceptance, such that, as soon as a season no longer serves your best interest, you simply lay it to rest, and never look back.

Chapter 3
Re-Define Your Vision

"Vision gives the imagination permission to exist within the Earth."

- Pastor Michael Todd

The million dollar questions we have all asked ourselves, at one time or the other, are, *"Why am I here? Where do I see myself in life?"* The answer to the first question is that we are all here for a specific purpose. The answer to the second question is what also helps us to move and direct that specific purpose. *It is vision.* What exactly is vision? The dictionary defines vision as *"the act or power of anticipating that which will or may come to be."*

What is Vision?

Vision gives us a direction, and a glimpse into our future, in such a way as to make our goals and purpose become a reality. In order to understand where we want ourselves to be in life, we must have a clear vision of our life. That is why, once we understand that our vision also clarifies our purpose, our life itself becomes more meaningful. It is so important to have a vision, if only because it will actually lead us to those decisions that will best serve our purpose. In other words, establishing a vision for your life will give you a direction in which to move. That is why the long-term goal that comes from having a life vision will give you clarity, and allow you to see where you are heading, and that means you can more easily control the outcome of your life.

There are three ways in which vision can properly direct us to our purpose. In other words, these are three reasons why creating a vision for our life is so important. *Firstly*, a vision puts substance behind your goals. Goal setting is crucial for achieving anything worthwhile. That is why goal setting is rightly said to be the *master skill of success.* In the absence of goals, it becomes more difficult to create a path to success. Yet, even with worthwhile goals, you must have a very important destination in mind. Your vision is that destination. Your vision is your end goal. Your vision gives you a larger purpose towards which you are directing the little goals you set along the way. Your vision is your *finish line.* Creating a vision puts meaning behind your goals. Instead of just setting small goals randomly, and hoping you will end up in the right place, your vision allows you to have a long-term destination towards which you can progressively move.

Secondly, your vision makes it easier for you to surmount the roadblocks you will encounter as you proceed on your journey. As long as you are making meaningful progress, you are destined to run into some roadblocks. If you are not struggling, you are simply not trying hard enough. But when you arrive at those hurdles, you need something to push you through. That is what a vision does for you. When you have something important to focus on, it becomes easier for you to recognize just how important getting through each roadblock is. Your vision will keep you focused. Your vision will inspire you to work even harder when those difficult situations arise. When you know what you are working towards, those hurdles will appear much smaller.

Thirdly, your vision sets your expectations. Success is often quite difficult to define. What is considered a success for one person might not exactly be a success for another. Knowing exactly what your vision is will allow you to set your expectations for your own brand of success. When you know what you want to accomplish in life, you will also know if you are getting closer to meeting your own personal expectations of success. Having a life goal can help you stay focused on your own path, and not on the path of those around you. When you know what success means to you, you can feel confident about the decisions you are making.

In the final analysis, however, your vision is uniquely yours, and that means only you can define it. As I have discovered on my own journey, there are certain steps you can follow to define your own vision for your life. Identify what is important to you. What do you believe in? What do you want to see changed, or what don't you want to see changed, about your life? Be creative. What are those things that will stretch you beyond your current limits? I recall thinking to myself, *"What are those things no one in my larger family has ever achieved? Can I strive to be the first person in my community to accomplish certain things?"* As soon as I started thinking in this manner, my sights for myself started becoming loftier than I could have ever imagined, and my vision became even bigger. Write out a personal vision statement. See your vision. Outline your steps. Create your vision board. Even if your vision seems far away, you should be able to outline the steps you need to take or the things you need to accomplish, to make it a reality. Try to outline what those steps might be to make your vision a reality. Let me tell you a bit of my own story.

Articulate Your Vision

I will have to quickly admit that at no time in my early adulthood did I actually sit down to articulate a vision for my life. In truth, my vision for my life evolved as I grew older, almost as if it was expanding with the passing years. It is true that as a little girl, I envisioned myself as a leader. In those fits of fantasy which are a constant feature of a young girl's fairytale existence, I often saw myself strutting on stage like a superstar. I would see my name in huge neon lights on top of a tall building, possibly a play theater, with huge undulating crowds yelling my name in feverish excitement. Quite frankly, I never really understood exactly what I was seeing at that relatively young age. Now, however, as I approach middle age, those fantasies are beginning to make sense, especially given the path I have been treading in recent years.

I do know for a fact that I started to envision myself impacting lives positively, and on a massive scale, for that matter. My own lifetime itself has been one of so much trauma, let downs, and setbacks. Yet, I have also weathered all those storms, only to come out gloriously triumphant on many fronts. I have always felt that it is merely the right thing to do by sharing the mixed grill of trauma and triumph that is my own story with others, such that, in some way or the other, they can become empowered for greater success in their own lives. I truly believe that it is safe to say that no one can ever arrive at their destination all alone. There must be people and resources who have been placed at strategic points along your life journey to help you reach your destiny.

Daily, I envisioned, and still envision, a life in which I travel from one location to the other, speaking to large appreciative crowds, with television interviews, magazine articles, and magazine feature covers trailing me globally. I have even seen myself anchoring my own talk show someday. Without a doubt, in that regard, Oprah Winfrey has always been my inspiration, and the person I look up to as a living affirmation of that aspiration. I cannot count the number of times I have dreamt of being interviewed by Oprah under her famous oak tree in her backyard. I believe that will happen someday. That interview might even center around the book you hold in your hands right now, or possibly, my autobiography.

I envision myself as a woman who is powerful and healthy in every possible way. I have struggled with my weight for many more years than I care to remember, and in my vision of my future, what I can see clearly is an attractive woman at a healthy weight, wearing a soft, white collared blouse, a black pencil skirt with a pair of black Christian Louboutin Red Bottom High Heels, stepping out of a black Lincoln Continental Limousine in front of the Apollo Theater, the famous music hall in Harlem, New York. My vision has chosen the Apollo Theater for good reason. For more than ten decades, it has been the pre-eminent venue of the performance of iconic artists across the broad spectrum of the performing arts in America. My vision comfortably places me in the league of these great Americans, as a renowned public speaker of note, and an impactful influencer on the lives of thousands of people. My name is emblazoned in dazzling neon lights on the top of that iconic building, and a screaming, frenzied crowd, stretching down the adjoining street, as far as the eyes can see, is waiting to receive me, in a scene that is reminiscent of the arrival of Whitney Houston for the Oscar Awards in the iconic movie, *The Bodyguard*. This is my vision of myself; accomplished, wealthy, healthy, educated, bold, and walking so much in my purpose that others will be sufficiently inspired to find the courage to walk in my footsteps. That is why a constant affirmation of mine is, *"Day by day, in every way, I am more powerful, confident, healthy and happy."* I would be happy, because I also imagine myself in a healthy relationship in which I am happily married to a man who is secure and balanced, God-fearing and self-loving, and who loves God first, and then loves me fully.

I am a change agent. I believe we have all been blessed with some unique gift or the other. I believe that I was created to touch people's lives. I also believe that God, in His infinite wisdom, has caused my life to be a story all by itself, just so that I can stand on a stage and share that story in such a way that it can help others turn their own trauma into triumph. My objective is simple. *It is to use it until I use it up.* I am certain that this will happen to me, and I also understand that, without God, nothing is possible, and that with God, nothing is an impossibility. With that understanding, I write the vision, and make it plain, and declare God's promises over my future. Each day, I approach the staircase that represents all the worthy accomplishments waiting for me to claim. Yet, I still have no idea when God will require me to take a leap. Still, I show up, in faith, in love, and filled with hope. I envision a greater life for my children than the one I have been subjected to. There is no place for poverty in my vision of the future of my children or my children's children. That is why my major obligation is to build a legacy that will last long after I have departed this Earthly plane.

See Your Vision

My vision started materializing in my college years, and in my early entrepreneurial journey. I had long decided to reach beyond my grasp. I had also taken the firm decision that the place called *mediocrity* would not be my own address and that I would consistently choose the prosperity, and the abundance, that God has ordained for my life. By the time I decided to add schooling to my job working as a bank teller, it was clear that I was stepping out of complacency and into the beginning of my path of authentic destiny. The phrase *'going back to college'* perfectly describes my action, simply because I had kept dropping out of college since I kept getting pregnant by my former husband and having children.

At first, it had seemed almost impossible to entertain such a big dream, but I persevered. Each day of that remarkable journey presented its challenges. Each day, I had to skillfully juggle my home life, work life, school life, and church life. The school aspect of my life was particularly challenging. I often felt that I was being presented with two options; be a mom and wife, or be an educated change agent. Yet, at the back of my mind was the unshakable conviction that I was born to make a tremendous difference. While I was in college, my family was faced with an enormous struggle. I worked at a full-time job in the financial industry as a bank teller.

That meant I worked all day, and then went to class at night. I hardly had any time to prepare proper meals for my children, or even spend meaningful time with them, the way I would have desired. Any extra time I had was spent completing my assignments. Basically, I sacrificed my family time throughout the entirety of my college career. Later, I would discover that despite modeling the behavior I desired for my children, my boys still resented me for hardly being present with them. Naturally, in light of the abusive marriages I had endured, I found myself feeling guilty for not focusing sufficiently on my children. During my time in college, we subsisted on Foodshare commodities, state medical benefits, and low-income housing assistance.

Seeing my vision materialize into my desires could not have been more relevant for the present times, especially in light of the global coronavirus pandemic. During the pandemic, like a lot of people, I had lost everything. I worked extremely hard in college and graduated with honors in 2019. Subsequently, I established myself in business as a motivational speaker. Unfortunately, no sooner had that promising career taken off, and been solidly booked for the entire year, than the Covid-19 pandemic reared its head to flip my life upside down. In a matter of weeks, specifically in March of 2020, all my speaking engagements had either been postponed or outright canceled, with only three booked engagements barely managing to transition to a virtual platform. Literally speaking, within a twinkle of an eye, I went from being solidly booked and paid, to zero revenue. Absolutely left with no other way to provide for my children, I applied for unemployment benefits. Also, since I did not have the capital funding to pivot my business to a virtual platform, I became stuck with a mountain of student loan debt accrued from my college studies, even as I had to contend with threats of losing my house and vehicle. Overall, I was facing a very real threat to the security of my family.

Yet, quarantine served its own eye-opening purpose in my affairs. Quarantined and stuck at home, I was forced to devote time to deep thought. In those long hours of idleness, I had no other option than to try and figure out what my next move would be. I recall sinking into so many moments of sheer panic and utter despair at the height of a pandemic that had thrown the entire world into a state of chaos and uncertainty. As soon as I came out of such moments of discouragement, and could think a bit more clearly, I would find myself calm enough to brainstorm on ways in which I could provide for my children, and how we could sustain ourselves in the midst of the entire despairing situation. I recall one particular day on which I thought about all my other talents, besides public speaking.

I actually asked myself, *"What else are you really good at?"* It struck me like a bolt out of the blue! I loved cooking! Very much like my mother, I was an excellent cook. My heart started racing. Many questions raced through my mind. *"Didn't*

I love cooking enough to say I was also passionate about it?Wasn't there some way I could monetize that passion? Where would I start from?" Suddenly, it occurred to me that I could pursue my passion for cooking as the owner of a restaurant. My mother was widely known as one of the best cooks in Mississippi. She had recipes for sweet potato pie, teacakes, cornbread, spaghetti, pinto beans, greens, cornbread dressing, lemon cake and so much more. At the same time, a deeply humbling thought crossed my mind. What better way to honor my mother's legacy as a great cook than to establish a restaurant that would specialize in all those mouth-watering recipes of hers? That mere thought of celebrating my mother's renown as a great cook served to fuel my desire to go into the restaurant business. That day, a seed that would germinate into one of the most successful entrepreneurial stories in my locality was sown.

I was thrown into a frenzy that shocked even me. My drive and determination were unbelievable. I spent hours researching and pouring into countless certifications, locations, and business planning methods. I consulted widely, and gradually started to flesh out the concept of my restaurant. I chose to call it *"A Family Affair Soulfood Kitchen."* The choice of that name itself received inspiration from the fact that I imaginatively decided to name every recipe after someone in my family. For instance, I had Mama's cornbread, Cousin Corylonann's pecan pie, Uncle Johnny's buttermilk scratch biscuits, Aunt Willie Mae's bread pudding, Cousin Daisy's collard greens, and Uncle Mike's deep-fried catfish. I also had my famous macaroni and cheese, deep-fried gizzards, banana pudding, and pound cakes. Working creatively around these recipes, I built the entire concept of my restaurant around my growing up years in Mississippi.

My slogan was also as creative as the restaurant's name. It was, *"Bringin' The South To Your Mouth,"* and that was because the restaurant, located in Wisconsin where I lived, was hundreds of miles away from my place of birth, Mississippi. The entire enterprise was a glorious entrepreneurial adventure that celebrated fortitude, determination, and resilience of spirit. Unfortunately, it did not last for long. I lost my restaurant to a tragic fire incident less than a year after starting the new venture. Although that loss was by far one of the most traumatic moments of my life, I still emerged from the entire disaster a wiser, and stronger person. I learned that as long as my faith remains firmly rooted in God, there is nothing so traumatic and devastating that He won't pull me through it. In my resilience, I realize that my vision for the restaurant is not lost. It is merely in the process of being envisioned as a new platform. It is written down, and so I anticipate that it will see the light of day, just as every other vision I have written down has seen the light of day.

Write Out Your Vision

The simplest way I discovered to express my vision was by writing it down. I believe that nothing just comes to you without conscious effort on your part. Whatever idea, concept, or vision, for that matter, that comes to you must be meditated upon, prayed about, planned for, and most importantly, written down. It is only when your vision is written down that it takes on a life of its own, and a vision that is not alive is no vision at all. It is famously said that the spoken word is ephemeral, but the written word is eternal. It is true. The spoken word, although it may not be forgotten, still goes with the wind, and can only remain in the memory. In contrast, the written word remains in material form, *cast in marble,* so to speak. The book of Habakkuk in the Bible talks about *writing the vision upon tablets and making it plain.* I believe that this is what happens to us in those times when we write on paper. The greatest way to affirm your vision is by looking at it, and you can only see what is written down on paper. A good friend, and mentor of mine, Dr. Alonzo Kelly, a leadership guru, would often say to me, *"See it before you see it."* In other words, you have an obligation to articulate a vision for yourself. You will need to continually see what it is you envision for yourself until it manifests as your reality.

Thus far, this has been the key to fulfilling my destiny, and my purpose. Writing down my thoughts and aspirations enables me to achieve a higher level of thinking and an emotional connection to my vision. My goals are of such vital importance to me, writing down what I envision for my future always helps to clarify any foggy areas that my brain might be struggling with while reminding me of what to focus on. If I am going to take the trouble to meditate on something, it might as well be my vision for my future. Writing out my vision and dreams helps me to extract the relevant information from my head so that it's not just swirling around in there. It helps me to prioritize, in the process giving energy to what is most important to me, while laying the foundation for the actions that I have to take to move my vision to the next level of actualization. Without this all-important process, I would simply become overwhelmed by the entire vision itself.

Also, writing down my vision gives me something important to return to. Reading my vision, over and again, helps me to remind myself of my life purpose, and why God created me in the first place. In the final analysis, writing down your vision is probably the most critical part of redefining your vision. The one certain fact is that you simply cannot redefine what is not written down. The habit of writing down your thoughts and vision also gives you an opportunity to express gratitude for what you already have. Soon enough, you will find yourself going beyond just writing your vision, and onto writing down thoughts of gratitude. Very much like the lady who inspires me so much, the legendary Oprah Winfrey, I keep a daily gratitude journal to remind me of at least ten things that I should be grateful for. Being grateful for what I have has helped me not to remain focused on what I seemingly lack. I sincerely believe that God blesses the humble and grateful heart.

Create a Vision Board

I have a very close friend. She runs a business venture as a skin care consultant. She sells products for the number one skincare company in the world. She believed so much in this company and its products that her enthusiasm was totally infectious. You could feel her motivation, and her energy, just by being around her. One day, right out of the blue, she asked if I would join her for a mimosa and vision board planning. I had never heard of such a thing. When I arrived at the venue, she had stacks of magazines, adorable art pieces, a whole lot of stickers, and motivational quotes, almost as if we were preparing for a party. Throughout the exciting session, we laughed and talked, and ate finger foods, all the while using all those materials to plan and lay out our future vision. Up till that time, I had thought that I fully understood the importance of writing down one's vision. That day, my understanding of creative visualization was taken to an entirely different level. Something special happens when you build your vision on a poster board. Vision board planning has given me the ability to truly, in the most simple format imaginable, express my goals, and what I desired for my life, in a graphic manner. I recall that life-changing time as if it was just yesterday. I recall finding the keywords and pictures that stood out for me in magazines, and tearing them out to paste on my vision board, all the while asking myself critical questions like, *"What do you want the next year of your life to look like? Do you believe it is possible?"*

I threw myself into the activity. Incredible as it may sound, only two or three of the items on my vision board remain as yet unfilled but are on the verge of manifesting. As I write, I am staring at that vision board that I created almost five years ago, and it is clear that there is a need to upgrade my vision and my vision board. I encourage you to do the same. Creating a vision board has helped me to realize that tremendous power lies in being intentional about your goals. Imagine the sort of progress you would make in life if you drew up a new vision board for yourself every year, assessing what manifested, and what didn't manifest, and continually redefining the vision you have for your future.

The most powerful takeaway from my vision board was the motivation it gave me to sincerely pursue my vision with conviction, commitment, and purpose. I strategically placed my vision board on a wall that was easily accessible to my sight, and where I knew I would see it every day. As each item on the vision board manifested, I would mark it off as achieved. My vision board brought my vision to life and simply became what motivated me towards action. I now had a clear direction on what I wanted, and the goals I desired to achieve. Once the vision was glued and pasted on that board, it became a self-fulfilling prophecy, since it also represented a definite sign that I would soon see it become my reality. My vision board sparked creativity, and it created fun, causing me to reassess my goals and reminding me that where I am standing today is not where I will be tomorrow. Vision board planning eliminates your limitations and inhibitions and gives you tangible daily motivation simply by offering you inner guidance that is both mental and spiritual.

Pursue Your Vision

To faithfully pursue any serious life mission requires genuine motivation. The word *'pursuit'* simply means to go after something without reservation. When you pursue your vision with total commitment, it will add *clarity, confidence, and conviction* to your journey of purpose. It is those three 'Cs' that will allow you to properly align with your life purpose. What helped me to remain true to what I envisioned, what I desired, what I created on my vision board, and what was written, was that the process of clarifying what I truly wanted was actually rather challenging, if not even intimidating. Gaining clarity is essential to know what you are pursuing. It is the transition from what is written, to a state of physical reality, that is ultimately responsible for the alignment. I understood that I needed to fully accept the process, no matter how daunting it might appear. A major crossroad I encountered on the journey of the pursuit of my vision was an *identity crisis.* It can be really difficult to clarify your goals, and walk with true confidence and conviction, without being clear about who you really are. I soon discovered that, while setting my goals and dreaming of what was possible for me were very important components of my journey, it was also hugely important to know who I truly am.

This, in itself, required work. You simply cannot execute your vision without fully knowing who you are. It was a real dilemma. In order to be able to redefine my vision, I needed to conquer that which was distracting me, and bring clarity to my purpose. The one message I can impart to you at this point in my narrative is that you should not be afraid to ask critical questions in order for you to become familiar with who you truly are. I found that I lacked confidence because, although I wrote the vision, I had self-limiting beliefs, and did not truly believe that I could attain my goals.

My faith is what carried me through those challenging times, and it continues to do so. I learned that the only way I could safely resolve my identity crisis was that I needed to continually remind myself of who God says I am, and not the lies Satan insists on whispering to me. Believe it or not, Satan is still in the infamous business of attempting to drown out the voice of God from His children. Steadfastly keeping my vision before God, and asking for guidance and direction, are a daily practice that has become a constant feature of my life. The best way to neutralize Satan's lies is by using the same method you adopted for redefining your vision. Write down the lies Satan told you so that God can give you a strategy with which to counter those lies.

I believe that God's promises are true. I believe that I can have whatever I speak to myself. I know that God will not withhold any good from me. I stand on these beliefs. God is always listening, and in order to fully pursue my vision, it is required that I stay connected to the source of my being. God Himself, in His infinite wisdom, formed me and placed His divinely-ordained passion and vision inside of me. Surely, I can only look and feel ridiculous if I go around asking all and sundry who I am, rather than reporting directly to the source to gently remind mc of my purposes, and to offer His unquestionable guidance. Indeed, I grew into this faith mindset as I traversed my years of failure, setbacks, and disappointments. I learned to trust what was written, and not what I was feeling. That is because, when all is said and done, feelings will always change, but it is what is written that will prevail.

Chapter 4
Step Out In Purpose

"The purpose of life is to live it, to taste experience to the utmost, to reach out eagerly and without fear for newer and richer experience."

- Eleanor Roosevelt

The word '*purpose*' has two meanings. The dictionary broadly defines it as the reason why something exists; an intended end, aim or goal, so to speak. It can also be defined in terms of one's life or activities. Accordingly, one might refer to one's actions as being carried out in a purposeful manner. A life lived with purpose is a life lived with *meaning*. That means purpose is what gives meaning to our existence, and it does so by offering us a sense of direction, helping to guide our behavior and paths, in alignment with our goals and objectives. In the final analysis, any reference to the discovery of purpose in your life is actually asking you to discover the real meaning for your existence. As Socrates, the Greek philosopher put it, *"The unexamined life is not worth living."*

Success is classically defined as the progressive realization of worthy goals. Yet, we also know that seeking success purely for its own sake and nothing else can ultimately render our life empty, if not meaningless. That is why we must seek a greater meaning or purpose to our existence, and our struggles. That means we need to live with a sense of purpose in which we dedicate our lives to something that is beyond us. Naturally, it also means living our life with such meaning and direction that we are inspired to make a significant contribution to our world.

We can find meaning in any form of existence, even a brutal one. Viktor Emil Frankl, an Austrian psychiatrist, and a survivor of the Holocaust was an example of someone who used his traumatic experiences as a concentration camp prisoner in Hitler's Germany to find new meaning in his horrific experience. In his famous book, *"Man's Search For Meaning,"* he wrote that the lack of meaning in a person's life causes a vacuum that can only lead to despair. In other words, we are driven by the necessity to seek meaning in our lives by committing to a purpose outside ourselves.

More often than not, it is a lack of meaning in their lives that drives people to want to conform to others, seek fleeting pleasures or demonstrate superiority over others. For most people, it is only after experiencing feelings of meaninglessness, despite their so-called successes, that they finally ask themselves questions like, *"What is the real purpose of my existence?" "Why am I here?" "What am I meant to do while here?"* and *"Who am I meant to be, and what am I meant to do?"* Mark Twain, known as the 'father of American literature,' once said, *"The two most important days of your life are the day you were born, and the day you find out why."* Although this is very true, we must all forgive ourselves for the difficulty we encounter in answering these questions. Benjamin Franklin once said, *"The three hardest things in life are Steel, Diamond, and the Discovery of Self."* Trying to discover the purpose of one's existence is not an easy quest. It requires genuine commitment. It requires effort. Most of all, it requires a certain curiosity borne of the knowledge that one's earthly journey must have some deeper meaning beyond a simple everyday existence. Yet, the greatest miracle in one's life is the discovery of the true purpose for one's existence. The second greatest miracle is the faithful pursuit of that purpose. Nick

Seneca Jankel once said, *"Our guiding light is our purpose. We cannot thrive until we discover it."* There is beauty in discovering this guiding light. It gives us joy that shines brighter from one day to the next as we encounter challenges and situations that reveal more and more about our purpose. The only thing that can guarantee authentic and sustainable happiness in life is the faithful pursuit of that purpose.

Conceive Your Purpose

When it came to the discovery of purpose, I was not any different from the average individual. I can remember the feelings so vividly; the emptiness, the yearning for something to fill that emptiness, the fog of confusion that threatened to overwhelm me, the despairing feeling of lacking, and the depression. They all merged together to throw me into utter despondency, and they always seemed to present themselves at the worst possible times. The simplest things, like getting out of bed in the morning, felt so heavy and foreboding. The best joys in life that we all take for granted, like being with family and friends, and creating new connections, all felt so unsatisfying. I didn't understand exactly what was creating these feelings, or what I needed to do to change them. It sounds almost like a well-worn cliché to say that one day something happened that changed my life forever. Yet, that was exactly what happened. Everything transformed for me as soon as I decided to focus on creating a definite purpose for my life. However, the process was not quite as easy as I made it seem. Purpose played a terrible game of hide and seek with me before I finally found it. Even at that, my purpose appeared almost unrecognizable when I found it because of the chaos that surrounded me, living a life of its own, and breathing its own breath. Even now, I often still find it extremely difficult to say conclusively that I have conceived my true purpose. Perhaps that is because the notion of operating in my purpose as a trauma recovery coach, professional speaker and trainer would come at a much later phase of my life. I had already taken so many different roads, and arrived at so many different intersections, before finally arriving at the idea that I was created for much more than I seemed willing to acknowledge. Grandiose as it first seemed, the thought that I could become an influencer, and a person who could have a tremendous positive impact on countless others, came to me when everything else I was doing did not offer me any sense of fulfillment. I distinctly remember feeling so empty inside of me and desiring to be and feel loved above all things, but it all just seemed so totally out of reach for me. As a teenager, I had been so exploited and turned to prostitution as a means of survival. I found myself searching for validation, and for fulfillment from other people, especially men with my father's type of disposition. That was hardly surprising. Tried as much as I could, and as desperately as I did, I could never earn my father's approval. As I grew into adolescence and came into contact with other men, my natural inclination was to turn to any available man to continue to seek that validation and approval.

It was merely inevitable that teenage pregnancy would be the result of my efforts. At the age of sixteen, I became pregnant with my first son, and promptly traded the need for validation by men for the sole purpose of creating a meaningful life for my son, so that he could be proud to call me *mom*. Then, I embarked on a working career that saw me employed at so many dead-end jobs. I began my journey into the workforce as a cashier at McDonald's, where I didn't survive for long. Soon, I started working at a company called Tuckers. Tuckers was essentially a hamburger joint like McDonald's. The only difference was that they were locally-owned, and not a franchise chain, and they served a fish fry on Fridays. I recall being several months into my first pregnancy at that time, and I would come back home on Friday smelling like a fishmonger. I tried so hard to wash the smell out of my clothing, but even the strongest detergent simply couldn't eliminate the stench of fish and oil. That marked the beginning of my hatred for work in the fast food industry.

After I gave birth to my son, I started work as a janitor at another company. I was soon fired for my inability to keep up with specified time schedules for specific tasks. Let me explain. I was afflicted with obsessive-compulsive disorder, and OCD, and would often become stuck in an office or bathroom that required a little more attention than others. I wouldn't stop cleaning and scrubbing until the facilities looked factory new. Naturally, other offices were left needing my attention. After I was relieved from that job, I went to work as a cashier at a local grocery store called *Pick 'N Save.* I absolutely adored this job. Its biggest bonus was not coming home smelling like a fishmonger. Additionally, I found myself totally enjoying the interaction with so many different types of people. I loved to listen to the customers' concerns and revealed them in the small chats they had with me about their families. The good thing about my stint at this job was that it made me realize I was actually a people-oriented person. Eventually, that inclination would find expression in my pursuit of a career at US Bank, a reputable financial institution where I would serve as senior vault teller for five years, before transitioning to National Exchange Bank and Trust for another ten years.

Although it might appear as if, in relating my work history, I went off on a tangent for a moment, yet, that apparent digression was meant to serve an important purpose. My story eloquently illustrates the fact that your purpose is easily conceived, and made manifest, in those activities that have occupied your time in the past. With each passing day, perhaps even unknown to you, life leaves you clues about *who you are, and why you were born.* In my own case, I gradually arrived at the realization that I genuinely loved listening to others, and relating with them as a kindred spirit. Also, that I felt the urge to compassionately offer words of encouragement that served to uplift others, was no longer in dispute. My true life calling seemed to be making itself clear. Quite often, I am asked how I eventually discovered my purpose. My response is usually very simple. *We all came into this world with the same purpose, but with different callings.* Our pre-eminent purpose on Earth is to glorify God on Earth. Since this mandate applies to everyone, it becomes a vital matter to ask yourself whether the career path you have chosen or the relationships you hold near and dear to you, bring glory to God. At this point, let me stress that I am well aware that not everyone holds as firm a belief in God as I do, and it is definitely not my intention to convert anyone to Christianity on these pages. I merely speak from a point of personal perspective borne of conviction. God has revealed my purpose through my relationship with him. I now believe that as long as I continue to consult God about His divinely ordained will for my life, I cannot fail.

I had so many career changes, possibly because there was a part of me that just did not know what I was supposed to be pursuing. My purpose was not always clear. I know that recently, with the global pandemic that plagued our world, I became truly uncertain about what might be next for me. Ironically, my uncertainty plagued me worse than the pandemic plagued me, even though I contracted the coronavirus myself. Permit me to paint a graphic image of sheer physical agony. Imagine yourself lying in bed, with every inch of your skin in excruciating pain. Contracting Covid-19 robbed me of all sense of taste and smell. Worse, I suffered a severe loss in weight, momentum, and purpose. I recall looking up at the ceiling and wondering if I was going to die. I could hardly take a breath without feeling as if my chest was going to cave in. I basically was so exhausted, and in so much pain, that a part of me simply wanted to give up the struggle right there, drenched in my night sweat. However, as I fervently prayed, and confessed what I viewed as my shortcomings to God, and then recognized that I possessed no purpose or power outside of what God allows, I began to regain not only all that I lost in my illness but also a renewed sense of purpose. After healing from Covid-19, I dived head-first back into my purpose. That purpose is to impact, uplift, restore, encourage and motivate others to become the very best versions of themselves, and I achieve that purpose by being a dynamic professional speaker who leads her audience with as much authenticity at her disposal.

Confidence in Your Purpose

Finally, I figured out my purpose. I started my pursuit of an Associate degree in Leadership Development at Moraine Park Technical College with a GPA of 2.53. That is not a particularly impressive score, I will admit with a smile. But then, I will also quickly admit that I was never really *the sharpest tool in the box.* Yet, I did finally cultivate the combination of self-belief, confidence, and determination that ultimately saw me safely through my college career. However, in the beginning, I was not only totally lacking in confidence, but I also did not have a positive support group of people around me who might have told me that I had no reason not to believe in myself. I started off my college journey with student success courses. Those courses were designed to help me gain some familiarity with the format of a college degree program. In essence, they taught me what the academic expectations from a college student were, how to navigate a computer system and its programs, and knowledge of what resources were available to assist me in traversing my college journey successfully. Naturally, as a high school dropout, my understanding of what all this new information meant was rather rudimentary, yet I refused to admit that I lacked that understanding. I believed that if those around me could complete the course, then so could I. It was simply a case of a stubborn refusal to admit defeat, and an equally stubborn resolve to learn anything I could learn, no matter how slowly or painfully.

I had a good friend who would always tell me, *"Arletta, I know you want to be perfect in school as you are in everything else. But, remember, child, C's get degrees too! Don't stress yourself too much."* Naturally, I didn't listen to her. I wanted to apply my very best effort to this college venture, and if I couldn't operate at the top grade, then I wanted nothing to do with college anymore. Soon after my first semester, just as the second semester was about to begin, I had to drop out of college because I became pregnant with my second son. I still wasn't married, and still hadn't found any measure of stability. Eventually, I gave birth to my third son and decided to re-enroll in the college supervisory management program. I felt that my instructor, Mary Vogl-Rauscher, was being particularly hard on me. No matter how hard I worked on my papers, she would still fail me over, and over again. It seemed as if I could never meet her expectations. It turned out she was merely pushing me to dig deeper, and to try harder, until I surpassed even my own expectations in the papers I submitted to her. She became my favorite instructor. That was because she did not shy away from failing me, just so as to motivate me to do better. I became pregnant with my fourth son, and once again, I had to drop out of college, since pregnancy always spelled a long stretch of illness for me. I went on to work at National Exchange Bank & Trust until I gave birth to my last son. When he turned two years old, I decided to enroll in college for the final time, with the firm intention of completing this time. This time around, I enrolled in Leadership Development courses and four certification programs. My previous failed attempts strongly motivated me to see my third attempt as a tough, yet worthwhile challenge. I was determined, and I was confident that I would complete my degree program this time around.

It was on this final stretch of my college education that I met the remarkable individual who would forever change my life. I met Robert Heyrman, and my life would never be the same again. Rob Heyrman was my instructor on the communications course. As soon as I came into his classroom, the first sentence he uttered to me was, *"Kid, you have it. I only meet someone like you every ten years or so. You have stardust coming out of your a**!"* He explained that as soon as I made my entrance into the room, the tone of the atmosphere changed in a positive manner. In other words, according to this rather insightful man, I am able to alter the atmosphere in a room by my mere presence alone. Rob was very much in tune with me as a student, and he believed in me long before I believed in myself. He took a profound interest in knowing what my goals and aspirations were for the future. After taking his course, Rob and I arrived at the firm conviction that I was born to grace a stage and share my story, in the process touching and impacting so many lives in my lifetime. Not long after this, Rob began to talk to others on the college campus about my goals. The college responded to his enthusiasm for me and began to create opportunities for me to be recognized and to showcase my unique talent. In my final semester as a student at

Moraine Park Technical College, I was nominated as Student of the Year, and asked to deliver the keynote address at the annual fundraising gourmet dinner. I was humbled and honored to accept the invitation.

That night probably marked the beginning of what I am now pleased to call my *stage-strutting years.* I never felt more confident in my ability to stand before people and make a lasting impression. I had confidence in myself because I knew I had sacrificed so much to stand in that space. I walked with my head held high, and my shoulders thrown back, and I held the audience spellbound with my story, in much the same manner Whitney Houston held her concert audience enraptured as she belted out the lyrics of her all-time classic, *Greatest Love of All* at the Apollo Theater in Harlem. That night, I received a standing ovation. Later, I was pulled aside by many of the guests. They asked what my major was, and what my plans were post-college. Their common refrain that night can be summarized in this sentence, *"Girl, if you do not become a motivational speaker, then you have picked the wrong profession!"*

Indeed, I had discovered, not only my passion but also my purpose. Speaking is my passion and my purpose rolled into one. It is true that the greatest miracle in the life of an individual is the discovery of purpose, and the second greatest miracle is the faithful pursuit of that purpose. I had also consciously identified the vocation that I would live for, and by which I would earn a living and a life. At this critical, defining stage of my life, what was of vital importance was for the music in my heart to find expression on my lips, such that the music will live after me, in much the same manner that Whitney Houston's music is delightfully living after her. It is because I have been able to discover the life purpose that I can now articulate, to the finest point of my own personal approval, my *Statement of Purpose.* That personal Statement of Purpose is *"I Live To Speak, And I Speak To Live."* I encourage you to look deep within you to define your own purpose and to write out your own Statement of Purpose.

To this day, it remains a source of amazement to me that when I began my life career as a public speaker, I was not that confident in myself, just as I was not confident in my ability to graduate from college. After all, earning a college degree was something no one in my immediate family had ever accomplished. Not only did I graduate from my program, but I did so with honors and a 3.98 GPA. This was made possible only because I discovered my purpose, and purpose itself requires confidence to pursue. Although I had dropped out of college twice before the third and final attempt to complete my studies, it was an urgent sense of direction that finally sealed my success, and helped me to discover my purpose. I finally realized that I possessed all that I needed and that this was the first time in my life that I did not require someone else's validation to celebrate myself and my potential. I earned my degree.

Concentrate on Your Purpose

Distractions are as inevitable as the rising sun whenever you are pursuing something great. I found my purpose during the course of my education, yet it did not come without a great deal of sacrifice. Distractions come in every shape and form. While pursuing my degree studies, my relationships often served as my worst form of distraction. Often, I was faced with choosing between going to a movie, entertaining friends, doing a date night to keep my marital relationship flourishing, or completing my coursework for college. College can make very exacting demands, and it is certainly not for the faint-hearted.

College demands a particular type of hunger from you. You have to hunger for knowledge. You have to hunger for a future. You have to hunger for much more than your current life can offer.

My desire was not to continue to live in poverty, and to not subject my children to poverty, was my primary motivation for sacrificing all that was humanly possible to earn my degree. I felt that degree was my ticket to a better life. It would be my ticket to possessing so much more than what my parents could provide me. I wanted to live out the wonderful scenarios I saw in commercials. I dreamed of a little mansion situated on a hilltop, with a very long driveway winding from the remote-controlled gates, up to the stucco-pillared porch. I dreamt of a heavy entrance door made from a combination of the finest pedigree of oak and mahogany pieces from the Amazon forest. I dreamt of beautifully furnished hallways and rooms, and a kitchen whose endless delights and possibilities only a great cook like myself could fully exploit. More often than not, it was these big dreams that brought me back on track anytime I wanted to lose focus, or anytime college assignments became so difficult as to threaten to derail me from my goal. When distractions reared their heads, I would fall on my knees, and pray to God, asking for divine guidance. Life never stopped happening to me, as the popular saying goes, in the course of my reach for greater heights, and in my quest to discover my purpose. There were times when my first former husband would overindulge in alcohol, and in a fit of uncontrolled drunkenness, abuse me. At such times, I couldn't possibly be sufficiently at peace to concentrate on my studies. During such domestic emergencies, for in truth, that was what they were, I would have to communicate my difficult situation to my instructors in as discreet a fashion as I could make it so that I could obtain the grace of extensions to turn in my work.

I recall once being locked up in the basement by my second former husband, knowing fully well that I had to be in class. An average class ran for four hours. After I had screamed hysterically for some time and kicked repeatedly at the door, he eventually let me out. I dived into the bathroom to fix my face and powder my puffy eyes and headed straight to class. The instant I walked into the classroom, the instructor noticed that all was not well with me. He pulled me outside the classroom and asked me if I was alright. With the wisdom of hindsight, I guess he did that because he realized that I needed to not suppress whatever I was going through but just let it out. At that moment, it felt as if someone had stuck a pin in a balloon to deflate it. In much the same manner that air gushes out of a balloon, I let out a wail of agony right there in the hallway, and collapsed on my instructor's shoulders. It had taken so much out of me to continue to pretend that nothing was the matter, while attempting to focus on my coursework at the same time.

All the while, I was literally dying inside. Once again, I was experiencing trauma at a very deep level, and for the first time, someone could see beyond the mask I was wearing. The instructor walked me straight to the counselor's office and connected me with someone I could talk to. Seeking help for my trauma was one of the best decisions I have ever made. The opportunity to share my grief and trauma with someone who wasn't judgmental, but truly wanted to listen to me, and help me find some meaning in all the chaos I found myself in, did a lot to help me successfully navigate those very tough phases of my college career that posed a real threat to my ability to sufficiently focus on my goal so that I could complete the journey.

Consistent in Your Purpose

Years ago, we used to encounter difficulty in locating destinations. These days, technology has taken that load off our backs. The GPS, or Global Positioning System, is a global navigation satellite system that provides location, velocity, and time synchronization. GPS is everywhere. You can find GPS systems in your car, your smartphone, and your watch. GPS helps you get where you are going, from point A to point B. A GPS has a starting point and a destination. By the same token, when it comes to faithfully pursuing your purpose, it is your consistent pursuit of that purpose that acts as your life GPS. As long as you are consistent in thought and in deed, you will continue to head in the right direction. As you proceed, you will discover that it is not every environment that can produce the good fruit that will enable your steady progress in the right direction. The good thing is that you have already decided *where* you want to go, and *why* you want to go there. The consistency that serves as your GPS will always ensure that even if you lose your way, you can always get right back on track.

Because of the *fire of rejection* of poverty and mediocrity that burned within me like a raging inferno, I was fortunate enough to quickly identify my '*why*' and my life purpose, and ensure that all I did, and planned to do in the future, were in alignment with that *why*, and that purpose. While I also realized that ensuring that those close to me, especially family, were aware of my purpose, and making sure that I secured their love and support to achieve it, was not a luxury that was easily available to me. There were two equally significant reasons for this. The first reason was that my marriage, while I was attending college, was nothing close to supportive. In any case, my spouse, obviously feeling totally insecure that I was pursuing a course that would make him ultimately appear inferior to me, did everything in his power to destabilize me, and make the prospect of attending school as uncomfortable for me as possible. Many times, it was just as I was preparing to go for classes that a quarrel would break out. He exerted strenuous effort to throw me into such emotional turmoil that, ordinarily, there was no way I could be in the proper state of mind to make meaningful progress with my studies. Only the combination of my *why*, and my *purpose*, allowed me to prevail. The second reason was that, even if I had sought the support of my own family, it would have been a futile effort, as they simply would not have been able to wrap their heads around my desire for a college degree. One couldn't blame them. No one in the history of my family had ever achieved that feat. To them, it would have simply been *mission impossible,* and so they were a no-go area to seek encouragement, and I didn't bother.

In these circumstances, I tried to help myself as much as I could. I would organize my time commitment to specific goals, and then commit to that schedule and attempt to make it non-negotiable unless I had an unexpected emergency to attend to. More importantly, although I succumbed to many episodes of emotional breakdown, largely in the form of crying and self-pity, I still somehow managed to learn to master my emotions, at least such that when my mind started to make excuses, I was able to use positive and encouraging self-talk to get around those excuses and remind myself of the joy I would feel when I had achieved my goals. Ultimately, I insisted on being accountable to myself, and my *why*.

Consistency has been the key to my pursuit of purpose, even in the face of all the abuse and trauma I encountered in my relationships. Showing up when I needed to show up was not optional. For me, it was simply a non-negotiable obligation. No matter how hard things seemed at the workplace, with family, with juggling the life-college career balance, I *showed up* because I knew if I didn't, it would sound the death knell for my dream of a better life, not only for myself but also for my children. My education opened the doors for me to pursue opportunities that I never would have even remotely imagined possible for someone coming from my background. For instance, graduating with a Bachelor of Communication degree from Moraine Park Technical College, an accredited college with a pedigree dating back to 1912, and one of 16 technical colleges that make up the Wisconsin Technical College System, gave me access to an even larger network of people who were also pursuing their own purpose.

Completing a college degree was a feat that was never discussed in my family. Education was not only a revered territory that was seen as beyond the scope and possibilities of any member of my family, it was simply also not a topic for discussion. The constant topic of discussion was survival. In the house in which I grew up, each day presented unique challenges that saw my mother adopting new, innovative, and strategic ways for us to simply survive. Having our basic necessities met was a daily goal. When I became an adult, the traumatic carry-over from such an indigent level of daily subsistence helped to firm my resolve to expand the future horizons I could foresee for myself and my children. The only obstacle I could see on my path was that paper called a college degree; that piece of paper that confers indisputable credibility on you, and compels others to hear whatever it is you have to say.

My education has opened many doors for me. I have been featured on the cover of magazines. I have been invited to deliver the keynote address at huge conferences, both of local and national appeal. I have *strutted my stuff* on numerous national stages, all because of one instructor; just that one *destiny helper,* who also just happened to be my instructor, saw more in me than I saw in myself, in the process drawing out the grit and tenacity that I needed to pursue my purpose at full throttle. Yet, I had my own part to play. I remained consistent in my efforts even when it seemed as if all hell would break loose, and the entire universe would stand in the conspiracy to keep me from achieving my goal. Even the entire exercise of writing this book is part of the consistency I speak of. Becoming the first author in my family is simply me, once again, daring to *defy the odds* in every conceivable area of my life, and to dream on a scale unheard of in my family. In the final analysis, I believe that when I have completed my Earthly assignment, and the good Lord calls me home, I would like the epitaph at my headstone to read, *"Here Lies Arletta. She Dreamed The Life, And She Lived The Dream."*

The challenges were inevitable, and they came, but I met them with prayer, and with uncommon grit. I continued to push through, and I constantly reminded myself of my *why*. That "why" remains my purpose pusher to this day. I know there is someone out there waiting patiently for me to arrive. In my heart and mind, I feel it, and I see it. I will not give up or give in because I know that God is with me. I believe that, since God began this work in me, He will see it through to the finish line. I remain simply in agreement with what has already been written. I am going to help so many others change the trajectory of their lives simply because I was consistent in my purpose, and consistency reaps benefits and great rewards. I am a living witness to that indisputable truth.

Commitment to Your Purpose

Abraham Lincoln, the 16th President of the United States, once said, *"Commitment is what transforms a promise into reality."* He couldn't have expressed that truth in better words. As one human experience after the other has proved, even though we discover our life purpose, seem to understand the true meaning of that purpose, are confident in that purpose, and even concentrate on that purpose, we are, however, not truly committed to that purpose. That lack of commitment can do terrible damage to our attempt to live a life of purpose. True success is simply not possible without commitment.

Making a commitment involves fiercely dedicating yourself to something. That is why, before you make a commitment, you have to think carefully. A commitment obligates you to do something. It usually evokes a strong sense of intention and focus. It may even be accompanied by a statement of purpose or a plan of action. Think of at least one major accomplishment in your life that has really made you proud of yourself. In my own case, although I can now think of many, acquiring a college degree must be the icing on the cake for me, possibly because it also allowed me to achieve a first in my family line. *Now, think of the initial commitment you made when you started on a project. On a scale of 1-10, how committed were you? Were you very committed or simply desiring something?* There is a whole world of difference between *desiring* something and being *committed* to that thing. When you simply desire something, you do it only when the circumstances permit. When, however, you are committed, you accept no excuses, and can only derive satisfaction from results. A commitment is a binding pledge that obligates you to carry out a course of action. Making a commitment to what you do, whether in your personal life or your professional life, is one of the most powerful principles of success.

As I discovered on my own journey, commitment is serious business. Commitments are powerful because they influence how you think, how you sound, and how you act. Unlike a half-hearted hope, making a commitment means that you seek solutions when faced with obstacles, and you simply do not consider quitting an option. Additionally, a meaningful commitment provides you with a script for how to handle matters when you encounter challenges. The truth is that everyone feels like quitting at one time or another. I cannot count how many times, with a child, I told myself I would no longer bother with school. Yet, I did not quit. Unfortunately, most people quit when they feel like quitting. An important characteristic of success is the perseverance that commitment demands. The temptation to give up will always rear its head. The key is to anticipate it and make yourself a promise that the feeling of wanting to quit will not overpower your commitment.

Commitment is the promise I made myself to remain humble and dedicated to the pursuit of my purpose. It wasn't always easy to stay committed to the purpose of helping others realize the endless array of possibilities that can be available to them as soon as they start truly believing in themselves, and begin to defy the odds in their lives, both personally and professionally. I took quite a few pitfalls along the way. I can honestly say that I have managed to remain enthusiastic about pursuing my purpose only because God continues to open doors that feed my hunger to desire to make a difference. With every opportunity I am afforded, to share my story, and to be vulnerable and transparent, I am strengthened even more. Of equal importance, the intensity of my past trauma seems to pale more and more into insignificance as I continue to speak about it and share my story with others. No feeling of genuine fulfillment beats that which you get when an entire stranger from an audience walks up to you, wraps their arms around you, and says with emotion, *"It felt as if you were talking directly to me. Thank you for being so brave as to share your story."* Such words serve as fuel to empower me for an even greater drive to commit to my calling and the purpose of my life. I often imagine the lives that would remain untouched if I had refused to share my story. Defying the odds is not an easy journey. You can liken it to walking uphill against a ferocious wind, with debris of all kinds being hurled at you with every step of resistance you bravely take. That is what defying the odds is all about. Defying the odds has been the Kilimanjaro Mountain of my life, and I won't stop climbing that mountain until I reach its peak. Even at that peak, I will not stop climbing, for the top of one mountain will always be the bottom of the next mountain, and mountain for mountain, I shall continue to pursue my purpose, and express that purpose, until I take my last breath on this Earthly journey.

I am both dedicated to, and overjoyed with enthusiasm about, my purpose as a change agent, because of the knowledge that arming me with a microphone on the battlefield that is a stage simply means someone is going to be encouraged and set free from their less-than-wholesome circumstances. Someone's life is going to be changed because they will not only become brave but will receive the courage to desire more for their lives and dream bigger, if only because I will be telling them that, although my own circumstances were grave enough, they did not stop me from reaching beyond my grasp. My enthusiasm stems from being able to provide a better home, and better living conditions, for my children. My enthusiasm stems from others' lives being changed for the better after listening to my story. My enthusiasm is at an all-time high because, I know now more than I have ever known in the past, that if I dedicate myself to my purpose, my gift will, in turn, make room for me all on its own.

Ralph Waldo Emerson once wrote, *"Nothing great was ever achieved without enthusiasm."* He was right. As I have discovered, enthusiasm is the energy; intense zeal, inspiration, focus, excitement, and enjoyment that possess you when you have a burning desire to achieve a feat. For you to be committed to a goal, you need to first feel enthusiastic about it, and its achievement. Your commitment will ride on the vehicle of enthusiasm. We would all love to do more and achieve more, with our lives. Every one of us has dreams and goals we hope to achieve someday. It had always been my own dream too, one day, put down my thoughts, and become the published author you are now reading. If we are to achieve a goal, we must care about that goal, and we must care deeply. Enthusiasm is required for this degree of care. The Wright Brothers could not have invented the first plane without enthusiasm. Martin Luther King Jr could not have led the Civil Rights movement in our country without enthusiasm. Thomas Edison finally invented the incandescent light bulb after more than 900 failed attempts. Only enthusiasm could have sustained such a monumental effort.

Why is enthusiasm so vital for achievement? *Enthusiasm keeps you focused.* If your life is like mine was, constantly inundated with demands from family and work while studying for my degree, then you are facing real distraction, and it is only enthusiasm that will allow you to stay on track despite the daily grind of life. *Enthusiasm helps you surmount life's inevitable difficulties.* There is no gain without some pain along the way. Pain is a part of the territory. You will face troubled relationships and hurt. Some people in your life will make unwise decisions that will directly affect you. When pain arrives, it is easy to become discouraged. Enthusiasm is the fire that will help you sustain your momentum in the midst of that pain. Without enthusiasm, you will lose steam. *Enthusiasm gives you the motivation to take action every day.* Achieving your goals and dreams requires that you take actions every day. Enthusiasm is the fuel for this consistent action. Those who work only when they feel like working, and study only when they feel like studying, will never get very far. A key reason why enthusiasm plays such a significant role in success is that enthusiasm evokes happiness. In fact, happiness and enthusiasm can trigger creativity, and they will ultimately help you to succeed. Challenges are inevitable on your journey, but since you will be creative, happy, and enthusiastic, you will be able to surmount these roadblocks. It has been scientifically proven that people who have a positive, happy, and enthusiastic mindset are more creative, and have better insight.

Another reason why enthusiasm played such a key factor in my pursuit of purpose was that being so enthusiastic about my goal, I was always so excited that I exerted my best effort in order to achieve the goal. My enthusiasm kept me sufficiently motivated to persist with my effort. My mind was constantly on my goal. I believe it was my subconscious mind that was actually focused on the things I was passionate and enthusiastic about, and when your subconscious mind is constantly at work on something you are enthusiastic about, you will receive excellent insight that will fast-track your success. Staying committed to my *why* has brought me to the presence of great names, and I am humbled and honored. Because of the sacrifices I have made to arrive at my place of rest, I believe I deserve to reap the benefits of this moment in time. It has been a long and eventful journey. There was a time when I felt I was worthy of nothing. The people that meant the most to me made me feel small and insignificant. My commitment to my purpose brings me, not only complete and utter joy, but it also demands validation from no one but God. How incredible can life be?

Character in Your Purpose

Stepping out by faith into my purpose inevitably produced certain positive character traits in me that enabled me to become the influencer and change agent that I am today. Naturally, most of these positive character traits were already in my possession and contributed to who I was as an individual. My character traits were enhanced as I developed the courage to give my very best in every endeavor, even if it didn't yield instant gratification as compensation. I am an honest, loving, humble, reliable, and compassionate person. This does not mean that I am perfect. In any case, perfection is a mere illusion, as there was and remains only He that is perfect, and He became a living sacrifice so that we could all be set free. The benefits of having good character in your purpose will sustain you when you are tempted to throw in the towel. Believe me, there were so many times when I second-guessed myself with regard to my decision to pursue a career as a trauma recovery coach and motivational speaking, especially since public speaking famously ranks as the number one fear amongst the generality. Who was I to believe that I could do something that so many others feared? Public speaking is feared more than death itself, and here I was, actually entertaining the thought of pursuing it as a career choice, simply because I believed it is the key that I possess to unlock the chains of so many others that are oppressed, suppressed, and depressed.

One of the most important tools I employed to develop my character was learning from people who are living the life I want to live, and who are already where I desire to be. The best decision I ever made was to answer the call that was screaming inside of me that there was so much more for me. I developed the courage to step out in faith and did not allow my economic disadvantage or my social history to keep me from reaching beyond my grasp. I knew deep within me that my life was meant to be far more fulfilling than working in a grocery store, or counting other people's millions. I needed to change my mindset, and by faith, pursue with every fiber of my being, the calling and purpose that God had designed and ordained for me. I could not accept mediocrity and lack as my final destination.

I was certain that adversity was inevitable along the path, and that I would need to bear down and persevere, but even more so, I was certain that God had never failed me then, and he would not fail me now. Therefore, I took the leap. I sacrificed so much of myself so that my children, my mother, and siblings could experience life on a different level. I recall the day my sister Belinda looked meaningfully at me, and said, *"Arletta, you are the Oprah of our family!"* She had no idea how deeply she had unwittingly touched me with that powerful statement. She will never have an idea just how much that prophetic statement is pushing me to do even more for my family. Ultimately, my journey has helped me develop the significant positive character traits of integrity, perseverance, grit, compassion, tenacity, stamina, and drive. As a result of the adversity I have suffered, and the pursuit of transforming my trauma into triumph, I am even more determined to never stop dreaming big, bigger, and even bigger.

Chapter 5
Rekindle Your Faith

"Say 'Thank You,' because your faith is so strong that you don't doubt that whatever the problem, you'll get through it. You're saying 'Thank You' because you know that, even in the eye of the storm, God has put a rainbow in the clouds."

- Oprah Winfrey

The word *faith* comes second only after the word *love* in the frequency of everyday usage. That means the word *faith* is a very important word, perhaps much more important than most people realize. Faith is an expression of hope for something better. More than a wish, it is closer to a belief, but still not quite a belief. This is because, while *a belief is rooted in the mind, faith is based in the heart.* We act in faith when there is no guarantee and no certainty. After all, despite the fact that no one knows what kind of life a child will eventually have, women continue to have children. Every woman has faith that she will bear a normal child and that her child will have a normal, happy, and successful life. We do not know how life with the person we marry will turn out, yet we continue to have faith that our marriages will last a happy lifetime.

Faith speaks the language of the heart. It is an expression of hope that goes beyond our conscious mind. Let's face it. All that we hold dear and precious rests upon our faith in people, even though their wholesome potential to contribute meaningfully to our own life is as yet unfulfilled. That is also despite the fact that the evidence of history tells a different story. The world is full of ugliness, brutality, and injustice. Yet, the fact that there is also tenderness, kindness, and concern continues to sustain our enduring faith in the innate goodness of our fellow man. Without faith in ourselves, we could never believe in ourselves and in our capabilities. Without faith in others, we could never trust anyone. Faith is the eternal water that quenches parched souls.

The story is famously told of a traveler who came across an old woman who was stooped over what appeared to be thin sticks. He asked the woman what she was doing. "I am planting orange trees," she explained. The traveler thought this was a waste of her time. "Why do you bother?" he asked. "You are an old woman. These saplings will take years before they will be old enough to bear fruit. You will be long gone by then." "That may well be true," she replied. "But I don't plant these trees for myself but for those who will come after me, just as those before me planted the trees that bear the fruit that I eat today." She was right. Her efforts were powered by a faith that sought to bequeath a legacy in orange trees for generations she knew she would never set eyes on. That is the mystique of faith. After all, Hebrews 11:1 defines faith *"as the assurance of things hoped for, the conviction of things not seen."*

Faith is Hope in the Unseen

Faith is one of the most significant aspects of our lives. It is faith that allows us to carry on when we feel all hope is lost. It is faith that gives us the strength to overcome any obstacle we face. Yet, it is not quite as simple as it sounds. How does one go about having faith in what one cannot see? As we make our journey through life, our faith is continually challenged. On a personal note, faith has been one of the major struggle points of my life, at least until I was able to relinquish my trust in my own capabilities and place that trust in the power of the one who created me. I know what I am capable of, and what I am not capable of. Yet, it seems I often forget that God possesses this knowledge about me too. The Bible is filled with quotes on faith, and many different examples of the demonstration of faith. What I have discovered on my journey is that there really isn't any definition of faith that can possibly surpass what the Bible offers in terms of clarity and ease of understanding. *"Now, Faith is the substance of things hoped for, the evidence of things unseen." (Hebrews 11:1 KJV).* This is a particularly favorite scripture of mine. I love this passage of scripture, not only for the hope it so easily provides but also for the *comma* punctuation that rests between the words *now* and *faith.* At the best of times, grammar can prove to be very tricky, and passages are often easily misinterpreted and misunderstood because of sentence construction. I choose to believe that the comma between now and *faith* is an all-important *"Big Pause."* The big pause is simply the gap between where you are now, *in the present moment,* and God's own appointed time for delivering to you that for which you are believing, *in the future moment.*

Faith is what materializes in your life as soon as you marry your hope to all that is possible for you, just because you have decided to *believe.* I have had so many instances in my life in which I decided to turn my back on what was physically evident to me, and rather, chose to believe in what had not yet manifested in my life. For example, while enduring the very painful process of raising my children all alone as a single mother, I had no choice but to turn over my struggles to God, and firmly believe that He would make a way out of what was seemingly no way for us. There were countless times when I didn't have sufficient money for even the most basic of our necessities, yet God never allowed us to suffer unbearable lack, just because I believed in, or had absolute faith in, God's ability to ensure that we did not have to bear the unbearable.

Quite often, very much like my mother, I would take what appeared to be inadequate, and convert it into surplus. If Jesus, through faith, could bless a mere couple of fish, and a few loaves of bread, such that these meager items of food ended up feeding thousands, what could possibly stop me from believing that God could take what little I had, and perform the same miracle? He performed the miracle for me on countless occasions, and the more He performed such miracles in my life, the more my faith in Him grew, for *faith* feeds upon *faith* to perpetuate itself, in strength, and in magnitude. You have a muscle called *The Faith Muscle.* In much the same way that your biceps muscles are developed and strengthened by consistent exercise, every action you deliver as a consequence of your faith can only strengthen that faith muscle.

Faith Can Move Mountains

You need to have the type of faith that will allow you to have a clear glimpse of what you want to achieve even before achieving it. The story is told of a large estate in Scotland. It was a magnificent estate, and its owner was extremely proud of his vast inheritance in land holdings. There was, however, only one problem. A huge mountain occupied a substantial proportion of his land. Naturally, that part of the land, because of the mountain that occupied it, was of no use to the owner. In fact, as far as he was concerned, the mountain merely stood as a monument to nature at its most ugly, since, if the land were free of the mountain, his wish would have been to extend the estate by constructing new buildings that he could lease out on rent. For a couple of years, on a daily basis, he would glare at the mountain, commanding it, with unflinching faith, to move. One day, a road construction crew came and blasted the mountain to smithereens. Why did that happen? What happened was really quite as simple as a miracle, and it happened because miracles not only exist but are meant to be believable. The government needed to construct a road behind the estate. The government constructed the road, and the estate's owner still had enough land for the expansion of his estate. *Faith can, indeed, move mountains.* That estate owner's faith moved the mountain away from his estate. Do you have to see to believe? No. In fact, it is what you believe that you will eventually see. This is the faith that allows you a clear glimpse of what you want to achieve even before achieving it. When a farmer of faith holds a few seeds in his palm and then looks out at his empty fields, what does he see? He sees the endless rows of golden corn that fill his field at harvest time. Real faith, the type that some people have, is actually nothing more than an inner vision of God's ultimate purpose in their lives. Most successful people have this type of faith at the early stage of their careers. This is why they are often labeled dreamers, while they are actually people of extraordinary vision.

Your level of faith can have a tremendous impact on the trajectory of your life. Your faith can easily determine your future, and how much you can tap into the potential and possibilities of that future. Being able to look at where you are right now, and then speak where you desire to be into existence is actually faith in action. I have been active in my faith since I was a little girl. I have watched God consistently perform miracles on my behalf. As we all know, whenever God does something remarkable in your life, its effects tend to reverberate well beyond you, and your immediate sphere of influence. Believing that God can move mountains in your life is easy when you can translate that perspective into actual meaning in your life. As we all know, God has control over both our *physical mountains* and our *spiritual mountains.* I visualize these mountains as those big, heavy, and seemingly impossible things in my life. If, indeed, God has control over our mountains, then most certainly, He can move them if we have sufficient faith to believe in what appears to be an impossibility. If our faith and confidence in God are strong enough, we can achieve just about anything we set our minds upon.

I have dwelt at length on my college journey. I will now address the financial aspect of my life. A college education is a very expensive venture. Fervent as my desire was to acquire a college education, the fact remains that college simply does not pay for itself. Even if you were fortunate enough to be on a scholarship, or if someone took on the burden of funding your education, you would still have to augment the funds from your own pocket. I recall how, by the time I was approaching my final semester in college, I had exhausted all my funds, and had nothing left to cover my tuition. I was well aware of the simple fact that I couldn't possibly pick up my cap and gown to receive my diploma if my tuition remained at a deficit. So, acting in faith, I applied for several different scholarships around my locality. I knew only too well that the probability of even being remotely considered by most of them was very slim indeed. Yet, I retained a firm belief that God had not brought me to the door of the accomplishment of my greatest dream only to abandon me to my fate.

I came from a background of abject poverty, and I was a struggling, single mother living off food stamps, and depending on statewide healthcare benefits for survival. Although my mother had ingrained in me the habit of saving for the rainy day, in my current circumstances, I needed enough for a hurricane. When God would intervene in my untenable situation, He did so in the most unexpected manner. An older woman in my city had been quietly watching me for years as I, a single mother, worked tirelessly at the bank to provide for my children. This was the destiny helper that God sent to me. She said that God placed it in her heart to help me attain my goal. I told her that she needn't hand over the funds to me, adding that I would be eternally grateful if she would pay directly to the financial administration of the college. I was in tears as I embraced the woman. She had no way of knowing she was the answer to my prayers. I shared my urgent and compelling need with God, and He exceeded my expectations in His response. Not only was I financially blessed by the woman, but the TRIO program was for first-generation graduates who sponsored the acquisition of my cap and gown. TRIO was given its name after the first three programs (Upward Bound, Talent Search, and Student Support Services), were implemented. The name is not an acronym. The Federal TRIO Programs are responsible for supporting college-seeking individuals considered disadvantaged. Many institutions use grants from TRIO programs to benefit their students. Among the many disadvantaged students, these programs serve first-generation college students. I was a beneficiary of that program. God moved powerfully when I needed Him the most. I glorify God for all my life victories because I know without Him, none of them would have been possible.

Faith is Confidence in Action

The two words *confidence and faith* appear to be quite similar. Yet, while they are intimately interrelated, they are not exactly the same. Faith is trust or belief that is not based on proof or validation. Confidence, on the other hand, is certainty in the truth of something. In confidence, we possess absolute trust, assurance, and conviction. In faith, we may find ourselves wrestling with uncertainty, yet we still trust and believe. It is, however, clear that to make the transition from faith to confidence is to enter into a state of full self-actualization. To arrive at this point of self-actualization is also to arrive at a point where we do not have to struggle for God's blessings. To arrive at the self-actualization that faith and confidence gives is to arrive at the point of rest.

My confidence in God has grown through the challenges I have faced. I suppose, just by virtue of being one of God's ambassadors on Earth, adversity automatically became my lot in life. Adversity did not spare me. It gave me little or no breathing space. As I write these words, I painfully recall how, on several occasions, I was publicly humiliated while I was married to my former husband. In those and many other such sad situations, I had to learn to rely fully on God's ability to see me through the discomfort that I had to endure, and not my own abilities. I soberly confess that life was particularly heavy and burdensome at such harrowing times. My second marriage produced no offspring. My four sons were all products of my first marriage. It is noteworthy that my second former husband already had eleven children with several different women in previous relationships. To the extent that we were a large, blended family, you might say we were supposed to be somewhat of a "Brady Bunch," if you will permit me to draw inspiration from the popular sitcom series that aired on ABC from the Fall of 1969 to the Spring of 1974.

My second former husband had major problems with infidelity, and although I am a woman of faith, I could never say the same thing on his behalf. We went through a really tough time for two reasons. He was up to his neck in debt. Secondly, securing a decent job was out of the question for him because of his felony background. Despite that great handicap, one day he applied to a local factory that was hiring and would pay very decent wages. I recall lying flat on the floor, with my nose on the carpet, and crying out loud to God to show him favor with that application. God answered my prayers. God touched the hearts of those who were in charge of the hiring process to yield favor on my behalf so that my husband could work, earn a decent income, and contribute to our household expenses. Once again, God had moved in a powerful way because I had confidence in His ability to perform a miracle on our behalf. My husband got the job.

Then, the devil got him. Barely a couple of months into that employment, and a wonderful source of income, my husband contracted an unholy affair with the cafeteria lady. She became pregnant. This is the age of social media in which nothing can be kept hidden for long. Soon enough, his workmates began to create fake social media pages in attempts to reach out to me and let me know that he was cheating on me with a girl that he had gotten pregnant. If this is not the public humiliation I referred to earlier, then nothing is. Everyone around me seemed to know about my husband's transgressions except me. I tried my best to give him the benefit of the doubt. Instead, he maintained and sustained his lie to me until the lady delivered her baby. A paternity test established that he was unquestionably the father of the child. This would prove to be one of the most devastating moments of my life. It was my faith and confidence in God that carried me through the ordeal. For a while, I was even ashamed to make an appearance at church, afraid of both the inevitable gossiping and the harsh judgment of those who would deride me for remaining in a marriage in which the ultimate betrayal had occurred. Thankfully, that ugly episode did not stop me from reminding myself of all the previous times I had faced similar horrendous experiences that were seemingly designed to destroy me, yet God *showed up* and *showed out* on my behalf. However, I admit that I questioned my own loyalty to God during that extremely difficult time. I just couldn't understand why God

would permit such a thing to happen to me. Still totally unable to make any sense of my husband's infidelity, and completely unable to come to terms with the devastation I felt in the circumstances, I filed for separation from my husband. Unknown to me, another tragedy was brewing just across town. The "cafeteria lady," and mother of my husband's child, had so badly neglected the baby to the point of starving him to near death that the social services department was on the verge of making the baby a ward of the state. I was presented with a tough situation, and I had an equally tough decision to make. My husband's son and her other children were taken into custody, with the ultimate aim of placing them in foster care. We were all mandated to attend court to determine what would happen next. For reasons I can't easily disclose, purely on the grounds of confidentiality, the child was not permitted to be released to his father, my husband. A week earlier, I'd had a rather unpleasant telephone conversation with the woman he had an affair with, in which she had retorted, *"You will never even so much as lay eyes on my son. He belongs to me and your husband, and you have nothing to do with this!"*
I was already embroiled in a bitter divorce process. Now, I found myself in a custody hearing. As if from some far-off distance, the judge's voice echoed in my ears, *"Would you be willing to provide temporary placement and custody for this four-month-old child?"* My heart, rather than my head, spoke, and I took the child into my care. I raised him until he was six years of age. A few years later, his father and I divorced, and the child now resides with his father and has never met his biological mother.

Faith is ever so easy to practice when you are cruising on the relatively easy lane of life. But, what happens when you have to tap into faith just to keep from sinking? My road has been one filled with the potholes of abandonment, betrayal, and tragedy. The ever-constant source of my strength is God. I have discovered that as long as I continue to walk in confidence towards God's ability, and not mine, there is absolutely nothing God won't do to strengthen me to persevere through my trials. I am a resilient and powerful being as long as my faith remains my guide, and my pillar to lean on.

Counteract Your Fear with Faith

Fear can easily bury your intentions. Fear is the greatest enemy of human achievement. Fear buries purpose, passion, and gift, and can prevent you from achieving your true potential. Your greatest challenge will always be the conquest of fear, and the development of courage. The wonderful thing is since anything you practice over and again eventually becomes your own habit, you can develop the habit of courage by simply acting courageously anytime courage is called for in your life. Courage is not the absence of fear. Courage is the mastery of fear. When you are courageous, you will go forward in spite of your fear. The Bible provides us with a remarkable story that illustrates the havoc fear can cause in one's life. That story is contained in the account given of how Peter sank while walking on the water toward Jesus. Peter sank because of his fear. Just as he sank because of his fear how many are sinking in their business and professional lives. Anytime I find my faith failing me, I simply recite Isaiah 41:10, *"So do not fear, for I am with you, do not be dismayed, for I am your God. I will strengthen you and help you; I will uphold you with my righteous right hand."* Ultimately, as far as your faith is concerned, the elimination of fear and the development of courage will always be the true test of that faith.

Make no mistake about it, you cannot walk in faith and fear at the same time. If you plan to walk by faith, you will have to release your fear to God. As we all know, this is much easier said than done. However, if you have learned how to endure adversity a sufficient number of times, you will become courageous enough to choose to act according to God's will, even in the presence of fear. The common refrain is that faith is the opposite of fear. I choose to disagree with that saying. It is my belief that faith and fear cannot live in harmony at the same address. You have to choose one over the other. It is either you are walking in faith, or you are consumed by your fear. Fear can easily hamper your progress in ways that you can't possibly imagine. Let me illustrate the fears that I entertained while writing this book. Initially, I just could not summon enough confidence in myself to embark on the writing project. Despite the many academic accolades that I have to my name, I still didn't feel as if I was smart enough to write an entire book, from start to finish, like all those other people that I have placed on pedestals of rare accomplishments. In fact, most of them have written more than one book.

Some of my favorite authors include John Maxwell, Brene Brown, Oprah Winfrey, the late Maya Angelou, Bishop TD Jakes, Joyce Meyers, Beth Moore, Dr. Juanita Bynum and so many more. While writing this book, I devoted some thought to the thousands of words they have written, and how much faith it must have taken for each one of them to release all that their heart desired to deliver via the message in their book. I am sure that many of them started out with the same sort of fear that I had. Even as I write these words, I am only too aware of the fact that I am on the threshold of becoming the very first author of a book in my entire family. Not surprisingly, I am very fearful of the outcome.

In all honesty, I wish I could gain total control over my trepidation. Yet, I know only too well that I have only my faith in God to rely upon. My fears are legion. I fear whether my book will attract sufficient reader interest to do well on the book market. I fear whether my book will be sufficiently popular to gain recognition where it matters. I fear whether the release of my story will lead to more and greater opportunities to touch even more lives than I have already done in my remarkable career. Most importantly, I fear whether my effort will lead to the accomplishment of the most cherished of my dreams, and that is for me to be interviewed by Oprah Winfrey.

Naturally, these are all fears of the unknown. I have decided to counteract my fears with faith in my ability to achieve that which I so fervently desire. I have decided that fear or no fear, my book is going out there to tell my story, such that my story can serve as a source of inspiration for whoever needs it. I believe that my prayers will avail me of the divine grace that I seek. I believe that God will place this book in the hands of those who might be struggling to defy the odds in their own lives, just like I did. I know there are people out there who have endured trauma that needs to be addressed, and hearts that need to heal. You may be the person I speak of. I believe, with all the faith at my disposal, that this book will be a soothing balm for your tortured soul, and that you will triumph over your travails. After all, if I could endure, and persevere through the many adversities of my life, there is no reason on Earth why you shouldn't be able to borrow a leaf from my strength to fight your own battle with faith also.

The Power of Belief

The human mind can accomplish whatever it believes it can. Just for the benefit of emphasis, permit me to repeat that in another way. Whatever the mind can conceive, it can achieve. The human mind is capable of achieving anything it believes it can. The key component in the power of accomplishment of the human mind is one single word; *belief.* The Bible says, *"Whatever you ask for in prayer, believe that you have received it, and it will be yours."* Eileen Caddy, a Scottish thinker, *once wrote, "The greatest secret of making something work in your life is, first of all, the deep desire to make it work, then the belief that it can work, then to hold that clear, definite vision in your consciousness and see it working out."* Truly, it is your deep-seated belief that will fuel your vision. In other words, your vision will ride on the vehicle of your unwavering belief. The key word is *belief.*

Your thinking controls much of what your outcome will be. Proverbs 23:7 in the Bible says, *"For as he thinketh in his heart, so is he."* Our thoughts are fully responsible for what we act upon. The reason why what we think about matters so much is that, ultimately, it is what we think about that shapes who we become. This line of thought brings me back to the dreams God gave me concerning my life purpose, and how important it is to meditate on my destiny as often as I can. I know what I desire, yet I also understand that if I do not ask, write the vision, reach beyond my grasp and walk in the direction of my destiny, all I may be indulging in is wishful thinking. What God has for each one of us belongs to us, but it is our obligation to pull it down from the heavens. God simply cannot release what it is that we do not believe in. I believe that if I think positively, positive things will manifest in my life. It is also important to keep dream killers and negative people away from you. Refuse to associate with those who would ever so casually assassinate your purpose, if only just so that they can continue to live in their perception that they are superior to you. You are worthy of all that you dream about. Chase those dreams in the full belief that you can achieve them. Meditate upon what your life will look like with the fulfillment of those dreams. Eventually, what you meditate upon will manifest in your life.

I once listened to a podcast episode of The Steve Harvey Show, in which Steve Harvey told his audience about all the leaps and bounds he took in life to become who he is today. He said something very profound. Using the book of Habakkuk in the Bible as a reference, he said his research on many successful entrepreneurs revealed a common denominator in their lives. According to his findings, most successful entrepreneurs tend to rise up at a very early stage of their careers, and, without an exception, they have a prayer life of some sort. Steve talked at length about the importance of having vision boards as visual reminders of those desires we have resolved to actively work towards. In his own case, he actually arrived at the point where he could conclusively say that he had implemented a list of three hundred items that he desired for God to manifest in his life. He read and still reads that list when he awakens in the morning, and before retiring to bed at night. Steve also took a picture of that list and installed it as a screensaver on his desktop computer, cell phone, and tablet. What Steve Harvey did was remarkable, if not even extraordinary. He kept his vision for the future, both alive and relevant, by physically positioning its components in such a way that he could constantly reference it on devices that he knew he was compelled to see and use throughout the day.

Steve Harvey's strategy for consistent present-moment awareness about his vision and his dreams sparked a flame of inspiration in me. I decided to do the same thing by replicating his efforts at visionary mindfulness. With the intention of drawing up a lengthy list of my desires, I became exhausted by the time I reached number seventy-five. Yet, I resolved that I would continue until I had written down three hundred visionary requests for God to fulfill in my life, with space with which to document the date on which those desires manifested in my life. I believe in the power of positive beliefs, not only about the future but also about the future of those to and with whom you are connected. That is why, on my list, I have desires that I have for my mother, my siblings, and my children. I am a firm believer in the benefits of practicing the habit of writing down what you desire for yourself and pairing that vision with your faith, and the unflinching belief in the ability of God to deliver to you in due season.

The Creative Process of Faith

To practice *faith* requires a creative process. Faith needs to grow, so that you will end up leaning, not on *what* you know, but on *who* you know. In order to continually rekindle your faith, there are a few practices you can activate in your life today. I use those practices to keep my faith in a continuous growth trajectory. The first activity is regular attendance at church. It is, however, imperative that you continually ask yourself a pertinent question. *"What exactly is attendance at a solid, biblical church home producing in your life?"* My answer to that question is, *"Attending church helps to keep my faith working in the right direction."* As soon as I discover that I seem to be running a little low on my faith index, I simply borrow some *faith* from those people who constitute my church family, and who can hold me accountable to what I am believing God to perform in my life. For me, church attendance is decidedly not about glamor. It is also not about claiming 'bragging rights.' Church attendance is more about being amongst those walking in the same direction as me.

My second practice for rekindling my faith is *prayer*. I sustain an open-ended conversation with God for the simple reason that adversity can rear its head at any time. When I cry out to Him, I definitely do not want my voice to sound strange to God's ears. I want God to remain in a state of constant familiarity with my voice. I believe that the constantly flowing conversation between God and me expedites God's response to my supplication, as soon as that response is needed. Cultivating and sustaining a relationship with God, and putting Him first in your life, will establish a firm foundation for your faith, such that it continues to grow on a deeper level. I don't know about you, but when I need God to send a blessing into my life, the delay is the last thing I wish for. Sometimes, when you are asking God for something in faith, the wait can seem intolerable. But, when you are in constant communication with Him, you will retain the faith that because God has shown up so many times in the past on your behalf, He will do so, yet again. That belief will be firmly rooted in the knowledge that God loves you, and you should have faith in that love. Of equal importance, your faith in yourself should be greater than your faith in the opinions of others about you.

Finally, I adopt an attitude of gratitude as a way of life. One of my favorite songs by gospel singer, Deitrick Haddon, is titled, "Count Your Blessings!" I could sing, and dance to this song all day long. Constantly reflecting on the goodness of God, and all that He has done for you in the past ought to increase your faith on a daily basis. *When was the last time you sat down to deliberately reflect on your blessings, in the process of finding new ways to show thankfulness for God's faithfulness towards you?* I love to write down all the things I am grateful for, so that I can continually have a visual motivator and reminder of how many times I trusted God to do something for me, and my faith prevailed. Affirmations go hand in hand with feeling and expressing gratitude. Your ability to have faith, and to affirm it, allows that faith to manifest strongly in your life. I can assure you that I am a living witness to this assertion. I am writing a book after years of entertaining the desire to do so. I cultivated the belief that I would eventually accomplish that feat. I had faith that it was possible to achieve the feat. Now, I am basking in the glorious outcome of that joint belief and faith.

Chapter 6
The Power of Forgiveness

"Forgiveness is giving up the hope that the past could have been any different, it's accepting the past for what it was, and using this moment and this time to help yourself move forward."

- Oprah Winfrey

There is wisdom in forgiveness. Forgiveness is your key to the kingdom of inner peace. Although forgiveness is vital for peace of mind, it remains the most difficult to achieve. The reason is that the emotional anatomy of the human heart is similar to the anatomy of the onion. For us to arrive at the layer of unforgiveness and peel it off, we must first, one after the other, peel off the layers of anger, sadness, fear, and hurt, just the way we peel off the layers of an onion. Forgiveness is the hardest thing for most of us, yet it is the most important thing we should do if we are to make meaningful progress in life. Forgiveness will set you free from the past, and free up your mind for creativity. Forgiveness is also the key to the kingdom of mental and spiritual development. Freely forgiving everyone for everything will make you a calmer, kinder, and more compassionate person. In fact, given my own story of trauma, I now believe that forgiveness is the greatest act of love you could ever do for yourself, and for others.

Oprah Winfrey once said, *"The grudge you're holding is actually holding you."* She says that for many people searching for peace and purpose, one of the biggest obstacles can be the struggle to forgive. This is especially true for those of us who have suffered trauma, abuse, abandonment, or personal betrayals, forgiveness can seem like an insurmountable hurdle. The journey to releasing resentments and vengeful thoughts, and letting go of the traumatic past, are probably some of the biggest spiritual challenges any of us will ever face. If we accept these challenges, the rewards are great because on the other side of forgiveness is freedom.

Being unable to forgive, most of us want to strike back, or retaliate, so to speak. Sadly, the mentality of retaliation destroys us, while the mentality of tolerance builds us. To leave trauma behind us to start the process of healing is one thing. To start to heal, yet remain ill in our mind, by refusing to forgive those who hurt us, is quite another. Not only must we develop a capacity to forgive, we must also cultivate an equal capacity to convert that forgiveness and reconciliation. Anger, hatred and resentment set up barriers that rob us of our personal power. Unforgiveness and grudges are nothing but a cancer of the soul. The vital question is, *"How does one set on the path to being a forgiving person?"* I believe that the first thing is to rid yourself of judgment. This is because you can never be in possession of all the information you need to make an absolutely fair judgment, and I know this will sound ridiculous when we have been treated unfairly. Yet, the truth is that there will always be facts hidden from us, and known only to God. In any case, none of us is so perfect that we can afford to be so harsh and unyielding with people who hurt us.

Secondly, you have to become a compassionate person. I agree that this remains a difficult thing to do when you are wronged since the instinctive reaction is to fight back and inflict hurt when you think you are wrong. This is where we must make a distinction between *kindness* and *compassion*. They are two entirely different things. Compassion actually involves putting yourself in someone else's shoes, asking yourself whether the fault is entirely the other person's, or whether you ought to take some share of the blame. Thirdly, you will need to creatively visualize the entire situation in terms of reconciliation. This means actively visualizing the relationship as healed. Picture the poisons of anger and resentment leaving your system. Allow your imagination to run riot with images of what you will accomplish with a renewed, wholesome relationship with the person. Fourthly, say a prayer for the person who has offended you.

These are very tough things to do. They are extremely difficult. That is because your anger towards someone who has hurt you is not only understandable but can even be considered very logical. However, you must immediately start to slant your thoughts toward forgiveness. If you focus totally on the shortcomings of people and forget that they have good points, it will be difficult, if not near impossible, to find any good and worthy person in this world. There is not a righteous person on Earth, who always does what is right always. Simply, by a conscious act of your will, refuse to hold a grudge against anyone. You cannot develop a great personality if you allow yourself to collect and hold grievances of any sort. There is an amusing angle to holding a grievance. The truth is that while you are preoccupied with your grudge against someone, they generally remain unaware of the extent of your negative feelings towards them. In fact, while you are simmering like a boiling kettle of water over what they did to you, they are socially busy partying, dancing, and dining. But, let us start the forgiving process from the beginning.

Choose to Forgive Yourself

You must start with yourself. We all have the baggage of self-blame we are carrying around. You must start by forgiving yourself. Forgiveness is a powerful gift. Yet, you must first embrace that gift before you can redeem it. Every one of us can recall those moments in our life in which we felt as if self-forgiveness just didn't seem possible. *What have you done that, in your own perception, was so terrible that you believe you are not worthy of forgiveness?* Often, just like anyone else, I tend to set unrealistic expectations for myself, and then go ahead to ice the cake by withholding forgiveness for my inability to meet the unrealistic bar that I set for myself. That sounds rather confusing, doesn't it? Well, in my case, that was not so surprising. As a young girl, I actually taught myself to set such expectations. I grew up in a house in which it seemed no matter what you did, whether it was good or bad, it attracted a negative report. As I write at this moment, I can recall so many times when I felt as if my actions always fell short of the mark when it came to pleasing God. I believe that I have genuinely loved God my whole life, at least from when I could comprehend what love for God actually meant. I can't recall ever feeling overwhelmed by the expectations God has of me as His daughter. Yet, I am certain that there are many times when I have missed the mark when it comes to expectations, although I wasn't overwhelmed. I know that God is love and that He has shown me nothing but love my whole life. Perhaps, that is why anytime I fall short of His expectations, I feel so grieved in my spirit.

I confessed my love for God at a very tender age in a little white, Southern Baptist Church in Holly Bluff, Mississippi. I made that confession sitting in a chair in front of the entire congregation, and was baptized outside the church building in a tin basin. I was only eight years old. Although my most significant, and very traumatic memory of that experience was how cold the baptismal water was, my confession itself was real, and despite my tender age, very much from the heart. From that moment onwards, my desire was to know more about God. At that age, comprehension of the bible was still in its infancy, and I relied heavily on my mother's knowledge to fill the gaps. On her own part, my mother's relationship with God was principally centered around her love for gospel music. I recall how we would always wake up on Saturday mornings to the stirring strains of the music of some of the greatest gospel artists of the time, including Shirley Caesar, The William's Brothers, Al Green, Mighty Clouds of Joy, The Canton Spirituals, and Truthettes. My siblings and I grew up associating the early Saturday morning sound of gospel music with two things; a thorough cleaning of the entire house and that mama was about to cook something wonderful, more often than not, my favorite meal of pinto beans, fried pork chops, and cornbread, and for dessert, maybe popcorn balls or a teacake. Do I, in my adulthood, miss those days? Yes! Even those Saturday morning rituals of house cleaning and good food, to the accompaniment of soul-stirring gospel music, ensured that the foundation in God was solid. As might be expected, as my life began to change its chapters, so did my obedience to what my mother had taught me, and what I had read.

In particular, I struggled to forgive myself for getting pregnant at the age of sixteen. I spent the entire nine months of pregnancy in pain as to how to address God or relate with Him, because of the disappointment I had caused my mother. To make matters even more traumatic, I suffered rejection at the hands of my son's father. When I called to tell him that I was pregnant, his response was simple, and it was brutal. "Why are you telling me? It's not mine!" He knew very well that I had been with other men, so he used that as an excuse to desert me during the pregnancy, even though I made it very clear to him that my son belonged to him. I struggled to forgive myself for desiring so badly to want to be loved, embraced, and accepted.

I was willing to give up my body for gratification, even if it only lasted for a moment.

Eventually, maturity helped me to forgive myself for that huge setback. Yet, the process of self-acceptance and self-forgiveness took quite a while. Sometimes, our level of expectations of ourselves causes a long delay in the process of pardoning ourselves for our faults. However, in the process of forgiving myself, I learned a very important and life-changing lesson. It is important that you refuse to believe that your bad choices, or mistakes, totally define who you really are. Thankfully, also, along the line, I cultivated a love for journaling, and that became a valuable outlet for pouring out my heart to myself. I was startled to make confessions in my diary, and since the entire process was an encounter between God and me, I did not feel as if I was hiding, either from myself or from God. Very soon, I found that I had forged a habit of confessing those areas of my life in which I knew I had fallen short in that diary. More importantly, as soon as I wrote down my confessions, they were no longer a burden I had to carry. Journaling also taught me just how much I needed God, and the forgiveness He graciously granted every day. To this day, I still use this process of journaling as a tool for self-forgiveness, and to help me let go of my faults after I have taken responsibility for them, confessed them, and written them down.

Choose to Forgive Others

Everyone deserves our forgiveness, no matter who they are, and no matter the nature or weight of their offense. As I mentioned previously, if we chose to focus totally on the shortcomings of people, and forget that, like us, they also have good points to their name, it will be difficult, if not almost impossible, to find any good and worthy person in this world. I have done some fairly terrible things in my life, none of which I am particularly proud of, and I certainly could not imagine asking God to forgive me, yet perfectly unwilling to forgive others. I take that command literally. In my previous marital relationships, I suffered terrible abandonment, immense betrayal, unimaginable emotional trauma, and so much more. Each episode of being cheated on, abused, or even abandoned by my former husbands, I still counted as worthy of forgiveness. I know that sounds really *crazy*, but I always said God created me differently. As a matter of fact, it seemed almost impossible for me to hold a grudge, or stay angry with anyone. There were times when I would cry out to God because of the pain of not being able to stay angry like everyone else. *Why was I so empathetic and compassionate towards the needs and failings of others, often to my total detriment?* My willingness to bend over backward to accommodate, and to go above and beyond the ordinary, just to receive their attention and the pain of desperately needing and wanting their approval was just too much to bear. I exhausted myself trying to conform to what I believed my former husbands wanted, all with the hope that, perhaps, they wouldn't cheat on me again. I was constantly disappointed.

What really took the cake for me was when my second husband had a baby with another woman and then decided, even after I had forgiven his betrayal, to continue to sleep with the same woman. To say that it was difficult is truly an understatement for what it felt like to try and mend that huge hole in our marriage. The rare type of forgiveness that I demonstrated was taken for granted, over and over again, until only its empty shell was left for me to pathetically stare at. After a while, I simply became numb to the betrayal, and merely expected to continue to feel broken. My consolation in forgiving my former husbands was the benefit of peace of mind that I received in the knowledge that God would continue to hear my prayers. I believe that, although I was the person who was offended, the real offense is between them and God. I just did not possess the capacity to carry around that type of unforgiveness in my heart. Even more importantly, I couldn't afford for any such unforgiveness to ferment and evolve into hatred, so I dismissed it as quickly as possible.

Forgiving those who have hurt you can be extremely painful, but the *Return on Investment (ROI)* for me was the peace of mind that God rewarded me with. Their offense was no longer an issue for me to dwell upon. Rather, the tables were turned, and it became their burden to bear. Besides, I had other priorities that needed and demanded my attention. Certainly, my children needed me more than my anger and bitterness needed me. In the final analysis, I refused to cave into the demands of anger and resentment because everything else I was carrying at those times also demanded my attention. Thankfully, those more worthwhile demands carried the day, and I was spared the agony of a festering sore of the soul. I will be the first person to admit that, as I drowned in my insecurities, I continued to be traumatized by the constant belittling and rejection I was subjected to. The thoughts still hurt, but they are forgiven.

Overcome Resentment

While I have detailed what I feel the benefits of forgiveness are, I feel that resentment is where my real conflict lies. In other words, my suffering itself lay totally with resentment. My struggle was not so much with forgiveness as it was my struggle with resentment. I have felt, and still feel, strong feelings of resentment whenever I am treated unfairly, devalued, disrespected, dismissed, or abandoned. There are countless times in which I have been resentful in my life. Believe it or not, the most resentful I have felt in my life was towards my father when he passed away. It is difficult to put the anger I felt toward him into words. My father had caused me so much emotional trauma that I eventually developed an unhealthy attachment to his mistreatment of me, and worse, I somehow went into my romantic relationships with that baggage.

I was so angry when my father died because we were both left with barely a few months to really get to know each other after our reconciliation. My father revealed to me that he had cancer in April of 2008. "Lettie, I am coming that way to spend some time with you and my grandkids!" Those were his words at that time, and I will never forget them. Although I was very excited at the prospect of his visit, the stark truth was that I was intensely resentful and bitter towards my father for abandoning me as a child, and for his relentless physical abuse of my mother. For me, that was a season of terrible internal conflict. While I loved my father very much, I was still quite resentful for all that I felt he hadn't been to me as a father. I certainly could not believe any father could claim to love a daughter, yet beat her, and mistreat her as badly, as my father did. It was when I needed my father the most that he was nowhere in sight.

My father made the long trip from Yazoo City, Mississippi to Milwaukee, Wisconsin. I was so excited, and I remember how it felt like Christmas in April. I drove to pick him up from the greyhound bus station and brought him back to my home. My father was a jack of all trades. He could fix just about anything in a home. Upon his arrival, the first thing he noticed was my broken-down lawn mower, sitting idly at the side of my house. He surprised me by fixing it immediately.

The feeling of Christmas was overwhelming. He taught my middle son how to ride a bike for the first time. My father attended church with me, and he played the drums and the bass guitar. He was an accomplished musician who had played the guitar for some of the best gospel groups to ever tour the southern states. He also had an extraordinary ear for music. Although he never received any formal lessons, he could listen to a song and simply go to the instrument to play what he heard. My son Moniteque Jr. is blessed with the same gift.

During the week my father stayed with me, I had to work at the bank, with no days off, for the entire duration of his visit, but he never once complained. On the Friday of that week, however, I arrived home to a spaghetti dinner and an immaculately clean house. Everything looked and smelled good, and the food tasted excellent. We had all convened in the living area to watch a movie. But, my father wanted to have a conversation instead. He asked me what had caused the distance between us, and he gave me full permission to pour out my mind without reserve. I did. That night, I completely forgave him for every disappointment he had caused me, and for every tear I had shed. I completely released him from all the times I had resented him for leaving me and choosing others over me. During that conversation, he told me he was sick, but he believed he would eventually heal. Unfortunately, despite only ten months of fighting for his life through chemotherapy and radiation treatments, my father passed away. I had never felt so much grief and anger in my whole life. With all his absence from my childhood and the trauma his actions had caused me, the reconciliation with my father made me believe that we had time to make up for lost time.

I became resentful towards my father all over again, this time for leaving me one final time. I had so many questions raging through my mind. I screamed my *whys* at heaven. *Why did you bring him back, only to just as suddenly, take him away?* I felt I would eventually heal over time, but each year, as soon as the anniversary of my father's death is imminent, that feeling of resentment rises up in me. That is understandable. We had made plans. We had planned for him to come back to Wisconsin for Thanksgiving, and he had promised that he would. But, the opportunity for a stem cell transplant came up at that time, and my father wanted so badly to do all that he could to recover. It just never happened. He never did recover. In fact, his condition worsened before he transitioned. He was visited with all manner of the unspeakable; football-sized boils, loss of all his hair, throat cut open to enable him to breathe, communication with only eye movements, and total loss of his voice.

While I resented my father for leaving me, I still rejoiced that his suffering was over. Although he had caused me so much pain and grief, and I truly lacked any understanding of the reason for all that, I didn't believe he deserved to suffer that way. I would have loved to say that I was eventually able to free myself of these deep feelings of resentment, however, that would not entirely be the truth. I suffered so much from childhood trauma, rejection, abandonment, and so much more, and whenever I think of forgiveness, the memories of my father's contribution to all that still lurk in the background. Yet, even my father deserves forgiveness. In any case, forgiveness is what God renders on my behalf on a daily basis, in spite of how many times I have disappointed Him. Also, my father actually asked me to forgive him. At our moment of reconciliation, my father alerted me to the fact that he had no idea that his choices and actions had caused me so much pain. I harbored resentment towards him for all those years, yet the effects of my ill will towards him were damaging to me, and not him. He wasn't even in the least aware that I was

129

beautifully broken. Here we have the baffling thing about forgiveness. Whenever we forgive, we do ourselves the greatest favor, and not the other person. We heal both our physiology and our psychology. We release ourselves from the prison of resentment and anger. There was so much I loved, and still love, about my father. I miss him very dearly, and so when it came to my turn to either hold on to the anger or let it go, I decided that God's grace was sufficient for Him too. I chose empathy instead.

Liberate Yourself from Toxic Thoughts

Many toxic thoughts have preoccupied my mind throughout the years. Most of them deal directly with disappointment and shame. Somehow, I cultivated the bad habit of pretending to be free, all the while hiding behind a mask of insecurities. Those insecurities were deeply ingrained in me as a consequence of unfulfilling and failed relationships, parental dysfunction, and grief. Toxic thoughts have set me back in life, largely because they are fed by self-limiting beliefs and self-doubt. I battled with feelings of worthlessness and shame for a number of reasons. The most significant reason was the extreme poverty of my family. Another reason was that, as one of the only few black families in the community, we were made to feel unwelcome in the community we lived in. I practically wore myself thin and exhausted in my constant quest for a sense of belonging. I feel I would have progressed faster, and been much further along on my life path if only I had not spent so much time thinking such very belittling thoughts of myself. I would have had more confidence, and more strength to really go after what I truly deserved.
If it weren't for childhood trauma, and my resultant toxic thought pattern, I probably would never have been exploited as

a teenage girl. I probably never would have chosen the men I chose to have relationships with since I would have viewed myself through a clearer and less foggy lens. From time to time, I still battle with what I see when I look at myself in the mirror. However, I have taught myself new habits that are designed to liberate me from these toxic thoughts. Whenever I feel negative self-talk starting to take hold of me, I acknowledge it by recognizing that I cannot be defined by those negative thoughts that are plaguing me. I take a step back to give myself grace, and to weigh in on the falsehoods that keep surfacing. I soon recognized that the toxic thoughts have less power over me when I acknowledge them, and then release them. It is not my intention to make the whole thing appear so simple. It took years of practice, but as they say, *practice makes progress*. Most of the symptoms of panic disorder and anxiety that I suffered through the years of my trauma have subsided, largely because of my willingness to acknowledge the toxic thoughts, and then combat them by sitting down with them and feeling them. I used to panic when the thoughts came, but now, I breathe through them, insisting on entertaining at least three positive thoughts to combat the negative thoughts. Then, I move on. I gave up too much space in my heart and mind trying to reason with the toxicity. Those thoughts simply do not fight fair. I would lose each time until I sought counseling help, despite getting and putting the proper medical treatment plan in place.

Indeed, I couldn't do it on my own. I saw a psychiatrist, and for a number of years in my early teenage years, and in my late twenties, I received prescriptions for Prozac to help stabilize my emotions and to liberate me from the toxic thoughts that trespassed in my mind all day long. I never gave permission for those thoughts to attack me, and as an adolescent, it was hard for me to express exactly how I felt, so

I learned to act it out in the form of rage, instead of communicating where it hurt. I have benefited from consulting with licensed professionals to help navigate my way through my trauma. Today, I am actively healing. Also, I am discovering what makes me happy and acknowledging my growth by replacing those negative thoughts with positive ones. The therapy sessions were really helpful. It was comforting to know that, although I couldn't always express to my father just how angry I was at him for his poor treatment of me, it brought me so much solace to know that someone cared enough to sit and listen, and to help me to make some sense out of all I had been through. Mental health is very important, and liberation from toxic thoughts requires a healthy mental state. I was willing to do the work. This is how you will become liberated from your toxic thoughts too. Do not be afraid to seek the help you need to evolve to the very best version of yourself.

Chapter 7
Reclaim Your Authentic Self

"The greatest act of courage is to be and to own all of who you are, without apology, without excuses, without masks to cover the truth of who you are."

- Debbie Ford

Being your authentic self; your true self, means what you say about yourself aligns with your actions. Your authentic self goes beyond what you do for a living, what possessions you own, or who you are to someone else. Your authentic self is who you are at your deepest core. It is who you truly are to yourself. It is about being true to yourself through your *thoughts, words,* and *actions*, and having these three areas not only match each other, but also work to support each other, and in such a way that everything about you speaks to who you truly are. It means your thoughts do not have an agenda different from your words, and vice versa. The very real danger of being out of touch with your authentic self is that it easily throws you into "people-pleasing" mode. As soon as that happens, you start to do and say things based on what is expected of you or based on social and peer pressure.

Being your authentic self is an act of courage. That is not surprising. After all, it is fraught with so much risk. People may not like you very much. Let's face it, we all want people to like us. People might simply refuse to accept the real you. Let's face it, we generally strive for societal acceptance. People will judge you. Let's face it, our ego resists what we feel is unfair judgment. Your feelings might get hurt. Hurt feelings, on their own, are a source of great pain. Overall, being your authentic self leaves you feeling more vulnerable to both the known and the unknown.

Yet, on the other side of the coin are benefits to being your authentic self. When you are authentic, you stay true to yourself, and who you genuinely are. You find yourself present in the *here* and *now*, since, being grounded in reality, you are not wasting time and energy in the fantasy land of whoever you might otherwise be pretending to be. You tend to do that which makes you genuinely happy. You follow your passions, regardless of who you end up disappointing, or how you may be perceived by others. I would be the first person to admit that living an authentic life is a *project* all its own. It is a project that demands constant and consistent effort, and it also means sacrifice. Not everyone in your life will respond well to your authentic self, if only because of how it may impact them. Yet, your project of authenticity gives you the opportunity to have others love you, and accept you, for who you truly are. When you are being authentic, you are also being vulnerable, and you are showing all parts of yourself; the *good, the bad,* and the *ugly*. The good thing, however, is that when you do this, you create space for more intimate, and more honest relationships, and you allow for true acceptance, and genuine love. Ultimately, your goal should be to work towards being more authentic, not being 100% authentic overnight. Becoming more authentic is a process that takes time. Anything worthwhile requires effort, and effort takes time to expend. Whenever you are in doubt about how authentic you are, simply ask yourself if your thoughts and feelings match your behavior. That is where true authenticity lies.

Hidden in Plain Sight

Renowned journalist, Matthew Petti, once wrote, *"Many hidden truths are often unobserved, not invisible."* He is right. Who you are is already out in the open, in full view, so to speak, for the whole world to see. In my own experience, being hidden in plain sight often simply translated to being overlooked. It meant being disregarded or purposefully ignored. While I was attending Sabish Junior High School, *tryouts*, or auditions, were held to select members of the cheerleading squad. I recall being extremely nervous. I was attending a school in which less than two percent of the student population looked like me. That fact alone gave me enormous shame, accompanied by a combined feeling of mediocrity and abnormality. Naturally, I was overwhelmed by a perceived need to over-perform just to gain recognition at a school where I spent the majority of my junior high school years. As the saying goes, *"black folks not only have the most rhythm, they are, indeed, rhythm in motion."*

Naturally, that also meant a perceived expectation to be an above-average cheerleader. That was expected because I was the only black girl aspiring for a spot on the squad. After all, I could dance. Also, I could build up the rhythm, and sustain it. Therefore, for all practical purposes, roaring success at the audition was supposed to be a piece of cake for me. Unfortunately, what they did not know was that the stereotype could not apply to me that simply. Unknown to them, I had *two left feet.* I was a country girl raised on country music. Dancing to a beat was simply not my forte, and it still isn't today. Despite these drawbacks, I was resolute, and I was determined, to make the squad, if only because that victory would translate to no longer being considered a disgrace to the human race, as one of my peers that *looked* like me would often say. He was hilarious. He would see me with my big purple glasses on, looking all *nerdy* and standoffish, and as soon as I got within a

135

few feet of him, he would scream, "What's up Disgrace?" He would say this so loudly that my insides would simply cringe from the acute embarrassment I felt. The fact that he was never alone at such despairing times did not make my ordeal any easier. He was quite the star attraction in any gathering and rather popular with everyone, he was always surrounded by a *yes* group of people. My impression of him, with his over-generous mouth and squinty eyes, was that he bore a striking resemblance to a ninja turtle. Clearly, I missed something in my assessment of his physical appearance, as the white girls obviously thought of him as the last word in masculine appeal. To this day, I can't, for the life of me, understand why they found him so handsome. Perhaps, deep inside, I shared their admiration of him, but his trademark words for me made me fearful of ever telling him. I stress this point because it was boys like him that made me feel that I needed to *hide*, and pretend that I wasn't *seen*, even though I was in plain sight. I think matters eventually got to the point where I sincerely believed that, as long as I could imagine being invisible, ultimately, others would see me as being invisible as well.

Needless to say, the heroic attempt to hide me from myself, and from others, did not work. It simply fell flat on its face. Finally, I mustered sufficient courage to try out for the squad. You guessed right. I performed well beyond my own expectations. In fact, my performance at the audition was so extraordinary that I was instantly selected by all the captains. If you initially thought I was going to say I didn't make the squad, I wouldn't blame you. After all, even I was in a bit of a shock myself. But, I recall that, on that day, the girl that was *me* that showed up at that gym was someone totally different. That girl; the one that was so conscious of *looking* different from everyone else, was someone gliding on a magic carpet with uncommon grace, unblemished beauty, soulful rhythm, and unmatched confidence. That girl gave the performance of her life, and the standing ovation spoke of the results even before they were announced. With the wisdom of hindsight, I can say that it wasn't so much the dancing that drew me into the squad. What worked in my favor was my yearning to be considered worthy enough to belong to a group of girls that I could hang out with, and be a part of, without feeling as if I was in hiding, or alone. My sense of belonging was fulfilled, so to speak. The stark truth was that I craved to belong in an environment where no one else looked like me.

As an added perk for making the squad, the school outfitted us in beautiful uniforms of red, black, and white. To obtain matching jogger outfits, we engaged in the business of selling candy bars, and as icing on the cake of our delight, there were bear paws on the butt of the jogger outfits! On game days, we all got to preen like beautiful peacocks, parading the school hallways in our regulation outfits of red, black, and white. Those were days when I would dare anyone to say anything negative to me. *"Can't you see I am wearing this uniform!!! I am a cheerleader!"* I was no longer hidden in plain sight. I had succeeded in freeing myself from the bondage of insecurity, and could now stand out to be noticed. My face could now be seen, and my voice was heard. The girl who was so afraid to be seen walking along the hallways could now strut the same hallways like a high school celebrity. Growing up in a predominantly white community made me feel invisible, even though the melanin in my skin made me so comparatively dark that I couldn't help but stand out. In the deepest recesses of my mind, I was *hidden, unseen,* and *unnoticed.*

My entry into that cheerleader squad would change my life in many ways. It was in the squad that I made friends that would become my family for life. Lynn, Kea, and my best friend,

Leanne, would help evoke my lifelong and profound love for the country music star, Shania Twain. Even to this day, I am capable of singing any Shania Twain, Garth Brooks, Hank Williams Jr., or Randy Travis song and not miss a single lyric. Those girls provided a place in which I could be free, and a place where I could be *me*. It took a lot of courage and confidence, but being close to those girls gave me the confidence I needed to come out of hiding, and show the world that I could really *jam*, even without solid rhythm in my two left feet. I was the one holding myself back all the while. I only needed to find the courage to become truly familiar with what seemed to be my imperfections and to accept *myself* for who I truly was. Ultimately, I learned that *perfection* and *imperfection* are but two sides of a coin. They are merely two versions of the same thing. That is why we must strive to be comfortable in our state of perfect imperfection. In other words, *there is perfection in our imperfection, if we choose to see the perfect imperfection.* I also learned that I no longer needed to be quiet and meek, but intended to speak to the masses some day, and impact lives on a grand scale, in total and unwavering alignment with my personal statement of purpose, *"I speak to live and I live to speak!"*

Own Who You Truly Are

"I am unapologetically me!" Is that even a remote possibility? Of course, it is! I have so many unique characteristics that set me apart from everybody else. It is almost as if my *presence*, as in my own *personality*, has its own unique fingerprint. I am convinced that there will never be another person like me. Earlier in our journey together, I shared how I made *normative conformity* my home. I wrote about how, when I was in elementary school and beyond that, I

struggled with such an intense desire to be accepted by others. My desperation to conform to what I perceived as the ideal was such that I would do anything just to look like them, sit with them, and be acknowledged by them. My situation was made worse by the fact that I was already so intelligent. Just to draw away attention from myself and my own brilliance, I would remain silent in the classroom, totally refusing to contribute anything that could possibly give my above-average intelligence away. Naturally, this was all in a heroic bid not to offend my very average classmates, and not to make anyone think I felt superior to them. I was perfectly willing to appear *average*, just to curry the favor of the *average* peer. I struggled with this tragic inauthenticity for many more years than I care to remember.

It wasn't until I was in college that I began to be far more accepting of who I truly was, both intellectually and emotionally. With every paper I submitted that earned a high grade, I gained increasing confidence in my ability, and I also gained the confidence to stand to claim that ability as mine. I always felt as if I had something to prove. I became an overachiever by accident. I had grown into the tendency not to see myself as intelligent because I had spent too much time in my adolescence trying to convince others that I wasn't intelligent. The image that my big purple glasses gave me of a *nerd* was one I fought with all the vehemence at my disposal. To be labeled a nerd was like being afflicted with the plague at school, or worse, being labeled with *cooties*, which, in itself, was like a plague when I was growing up.

Among children, cooties are an imaginary *germ*, with which a socially undesirable person is said to be infected. If someone as much as said you had cooties, you might as well just disappear into the abyss since everyone would avoid you to avoid those cooties jumping off on them. I definitely did not have cooties; I was black. I was unique. I was brilliant. The only unfortunate thing was that I didn't know it yet, and those around me refused to tell me so either. Sadly for me, on a personal note, not only did I wear big purple glasses and was considered a nerd, but I was also a bit overweight. That was to be expected. I would overindulge in extra treats to compensate for my deep feelings of inner hurt. There was little or no room for self-discipline because I was busy fighting off the other demons that haunted me on a daily basis. I would hang out in the cafeteria, long after the lunch hour ended. With everyone going on recess, I would linger, near the cafeteria ladies. With my inborn skills at being polite, cordial, and respectful, I charmed those ladies to no end, and would be rewarded with more delicious desserts, and sometimes, even an extra slice of pizza. I went out of my way to make them smile and feel appreciated. Besides, I came from a low-income family, and many of the delectable snacks I received at school were not necessarily available at home. That is not to play down my mother's magic touch at making a meal filling and delicious. I was blessed to have a mother who made the best of what was available, to provide what was necessary for the best possible way. It was just that I craved more at the cafeteria to assuage a deep, inner turmoil.

The journey to learning to take ownership of the true depth of who I am started much later in life because I had issues; *daddy issues, abandonment issues, low self-esteem issues, and so much more.* I spent the greater part of my adolescent years searching for my identity, and for validation from others. By the time I emerged into adulthood, I had already graduated from being exploited by older men, to parading myself around, looking for someone to love, until finally, I found God once again, and allowed what He said about me to become the report that I believed. I can now declare that I am a *peculiar princess*. I am the daughter of the King. I am unique, and beautifully and marvelously made.

Therefore, I no longer have to waste time pretending to be someone else. These days, I often say that one of my superpowers is my authenticity. Showing up unapologetically as I am is my new expertise. I spent too many years living in conformity, and when I finally broke free of that bondage, it was to never return to settling for anything less than what God called me to be. I now live each day in the rich fullness of my purpose, while also assisting others to take full ownership of their own authenticity. While the world will always have its celebrities, each one of us is a celebrity of our own life. We must write the script of our own life, own the script of the movie of that life, direct that movie, and play the starring role in the movie. That is how to own yourself, and your own story. I will always be the leading lady in my own story. Ultimately, you and I are called to stop accepting to be extras on the movie set, and to step forward to, rather, accept the starring role in the movie of our life. That is the only thing that can truly justify the esteemed role we are invited to play as children of a mighty and awesome God.

Self-Acceptance is Self-Power

Today, I am in a position to say that my wounds, flaws, and scars have all combined to make me the marvelous creature I have become. They have also empowered me to take that vital step forward to learn what true authenticity means. I have also arrived at an understanding of the vital importance of choosing, on a daily basis, to accept the truth of who I am without fading into the background because of my perceived inadequacies, or because of the intimidation I felt when I found myself in certain rooms. There were many occasions in the past when I felt undeserving until I started to discover, much to my surprise, that even the seemingly most confident person in the room is burdened with their own insecurities, and that they merely only mask them very well. That particular skill is one I have never really mastered.

I recall that my mother would often say that I wore my heart on my sleeve. She never had to ask me how something made me feel because, no matter how hard I tried to mask the pain, it would simply run out of my eyes and down my cheeks, each and every single time. I am prone to extremely deep and intense emotions. In loving others, I always had the expectation that my love would be reciprocated with the same energy I brought into the relationship. I was wrong every single time. To my utter dismay, I discovered that, generally, people are only capable of loving you with the same capacity, and with the same intensity, with which they love themselves. I believe that people who abuse others and cause harm to others, are merely reflecting what they were helplessly subjected to in the past, or they just simply have a deep-seated hatred for themselves that they are expressing through their abusive conduct.

I soon learned not to take rejection personally, especially by my loved ones. I found that they actually loved me, it was just that the love came from a place that was empty and dark within them. Although I was in pain, I vowed not to withhold my love, despite having to struggle with my own self-acceptance. I truly struggled to accept the totality of *my true self* because my foundation in love was weak. It was built on a very flimsy foundation. I seemed to be constantly in search of an elusive sense of belonging that seemed nearly impossible to obtain. It wasn't until I began to build up my faith and assume the identity that God prepared for me, that my confidence started to increase. I was lacking in confidence, but God is intentional about turning mediocre into something masterful and brilliant. The closer I drew to God, the more confident I became in my ability to overcome adversity. I knew I wasn't working for myself, but that it was God working through me. Eventually, self-acceptance became one of my many superpowers because it drove me to help others to be intentional about tapping into their strengths and celebrating them, rather than focusing on their weaknesses.

I am now a social media influencer because of the self-power I have derived from accepting myself, and I use that self-power to inspire others. My platform of influence is now utilized to assist others to deal with those traumatic events that have shaped their lives, such that they can truly address those unfortunate events, unburden themselves of the baggage they represent, and then bask in the warm knowledge of no longer trudging wearily on the journey, all alone. Never in my wildest dream could I have ever imagined that God would use exactly what I loathed about my own past and journey to inspire change in others. Self-acceptance is my self-power. Each passing day, I am reminded that it is God working through me to make my life impactful and that I cannot take credit for what I have been able to achieve in the lives of others. I have been simply awed and honored just to watch as I transitioned from my *prison of reproach* to my *palace of fulfillment,* after so many years of feeling insignificant and overlooked. It wasn't until I accepted *myself that* I found my own locus of relevance in the world. I expressed this clearly in my TEDx talk, *"Creating The Awe In Your Authenticity,"* by firmly stating that if you choose to accept yourself and your authenticity, the world will do so as well.

Embrace Your Self-Worth

I spent so many years of my life feeling so unworthy and undervalued that this new love walk feels totally surreal. I always say that God blesses me with material things, not only because I have a taste in all things beautiful and refined, but also because God can trust me with them. I may possess material things, but those things do not possess me. I possess my possessions, and not the other way round. I urge you to read that statement repeatedly, so that it sinks into your consciousness. I may have material things, but those things do not have me. *I possess my possessions. My possessions do not possess me.* God is my everything. Let me explain. If I lost everything I have, I would still have everything I need. Let me repeat that. *If I lost everything I have, I would still have everything I need. That is simply because God is my everything, and He is everything I need.* My very existence and being is wrapped up in the *One* who created me. I have no confidence in the things of this world. *I may be in this world, but I am not of this world.* In their bare essence, the material things of this world, and even our human existence, may be here today, yet gone tomorrow.

I have incurred so many losses over my lifetime that I no longer cling to things. In other words, I have become immune to materialism. While, just like anybody else, I desire financial security, existential stability, and material self-sufficiency, I have come to view it all from the perspective of my reliance on God to take care of me and provide for me. I am convinced that nothing is possible without that relationship. That is simply how I see it, and I am unapologetic about it. I cast my mind back over the many storms in life that I have endured, and I am still taken aback that my *chariot of fate* has still managed to arrive at its destination, my place of rest. The enemy of my soul has tried all in its limited power to defeat me, but my unflinching faith in God's ability, rather than my own capacity, has all but assured me that I cannot fail. I am destined to succeed and succeed I will.

I have been able to embrace my self-worth because God has counted me as worthy. I deserve everything good that happens to me and for me. I deserve all the accolades and acknowledgments that come my way because I came through a raging hell wearing only a pair of flimsy underwear soaked in gasoline, and emerged after the storm achieving my long list of accomplishments. Many people believe that wealth speaks only about money. I view wealth from a broader perspective. I am wealthy in so many different areas besides mammon. I am wealthy in love, gratitude, attitude, connection, authenticity, relatability, vulnerability, and transparency. Above all these, I have wealth of wisdom, and of knowledge. I have so much more to contribute beyond a *dollar*. Despondent as that might sound to many, the American dollar and its value will eventually fade away, and what will be left of me is all that I have stored up in places above, and not beneath. Whatever anyone may say to the contrary, I feel that I am worthy of the best things this life has to offer. Everything I possess was forged in a fire that was a deliberate sacrifice. Nothing was ever handed to me on a platter of gold. I am definitely not the worst for my sacrifice and struggle, as those things that I possess actually have much greater value than if they had just been handed over to me as gifts or charity. While I can, in gratitude, recall a few instances when God allowed people to bless me along my journey, the long stretch of that journey has seen me standing on my feet for long days and long hours, only to provide mediocre earnings that were only barely enough to sustain me and mine. Yet, every dollar was made to stretch itself out to sustain me and my entire household. *I am worthy, not because of who I am, but because of whose I am.* My heart stays filled with gratitude for what God has already done, in contrast with what I feel I am lacking.

I have a word of advice for you. Build your self-worth by doing those things that seem beyond your grasp. Be confident and strong in might, and in tenacity. Be willing to work hard and smart, and to depend solely on God, and not individuals. God is your only constant source of survival. Establish your self-worth by breaking a generational curse of ignorance and mediocrity by getting an education. Keep a safe distance from negative words and negative people. If you see something you would love to possess, and it is within your means to do so, by all means, buy it. You will only live this single lifetime, and at the end of your days, you will not take your money with you. You will never see a hearse pulling a house, or a bank vault bursting at the seams with dollars. Therefore, you are better off setting your sights on what is above and worrying less about what is beneath. Treat the people God has brought into your life in this season with love and respect, as this is the healthiest and best reflection of you as you prepare to fully embrace your self-worth.

Break Free of Labels

I broke free from demeaning labels and found solace in relabeling myself. I detached myself from what the world called me; a mere, marginalized statistic. I detached myself from what my father called me; stupid, whore, slut, dumb, a burden, and no daughter of his. I detached myself from the labels that my former spouses attached to me; ignorant, not enough, unworthy, evil, demonic, low down, goody two shoes, stuck up, lonely, needy, hard to love and so much more that I absolutely refuse to dignify with further space in this book. More significantly, I detach from the negative labels I gave myself; ugly, fat, too black, too dark, naïve, unlovable, and the rest of the uncomplimentary terms I unwisely chose to color myself in my past, and with which I beat down on my fragile self-esteem. When others constantly call you everything but a child of God, it can be extremely difficult to believe that you possess any redeeming feature whatsoever. I literally had to go through a long and arduous journey of self-discovery to break free from the labels with which I was bound. I learned the hard way that it is only the positive labels you give yourself that matter in the long run, and you have to work hard to firmly establish that self-talk as your own personal point of reference. One of the ways in which I broke free of the labels my former spouses gave me was by engaging in *mirror talk*. Simple as I might make it sound, I can assure you that nothing is more tiresome and tiring than a grueling domestic argument and brutal marital war, and it can be truly hard to gather together what is left of your self-possession, and shut yourself off in the bathroom or your bedroom, in a brave attempt to build back what had been torn into shreds. Sometimes, I even helplessly agreed with the labels they gave me. It was largely a landscape of manipulation and abuse, and little else. The repetitive verbal abuse finally broke into my subconscious and mental realm and stole all my dignity and pride. Most of the time, they would tear into me with all the verbal viciousness at their disposal, and then I would finish myself off with an extra layer of negative self-talk.

It took me years to break free of the toxicity, composed of both the poison of other people and the venom of my own self-talk. In the final analysis, my craving to become an overachiever, as a way of compensating for my unspeakable trauma, probably saved me from total destruction. It turned out that it wasn't possible to be considered stupid, dumb, or ignorant, with all these degrees I have hanging on my wall.

Those accomplishments rendered their reports null and void. I may not have been the daughter my father wanted, but my heavenly father stepped in to take his place. I will always be a girl who loves her God, and the apple of His eye. I was never unworthy or unlovable. I merely viewed myself through someone else's foggy lenses. All I needed to do, which I did, was to remove the rose-colored glasses and the labels and to establish a safe distance from those who had attached those labels, and the process of evolving into the true essence of who I am began in earnest. The new *me* glows like a newly-cut diamond with my new labels. I have finally reclaimed my authentic self. I am now whole. I am loved. I am a rare work of art. I am unique. I am intelligent. I am kind. I am loving. I am compassionate. I am confident. I am relatable. I am resilient. I am transparent. I am vulnerable. I am inspirational. I am a change agent. I am dynamic. I am beautiful. I am strong. I am defying the odds every day. I am the rich daughter of a rich God. I am *me*; the authentic *me*.

Chapter 8
Invest in Yourself

"The best gift you can give to yourself is to invest in yourself."

- Pooja Agnihotri

Investing in yourself can be one of the easiest, cheapest, and most rewarding benefits of your time. *By starting to make small changes to your life today, you can create higher returns for your future.* As you start investing in yourself, you will soon realize that you are making an impact on others around you as well. Investing in yourself means putting in the time, money, and energy into improving your current and future life. Instead of focusing on things that will not increase your overall long term worth, in terms of both *affluence* and *influence*, look for ways to expand your knowledge in order to make your life better. When you focus on improving yourself and reaching your goals, you will notice a positive overall effect on your finances, career, health, and happiness.

Why it is Important to Invest in Yourself

When you invest in yourself, you gain knowledge and skills that lower the amount of time you focus on things that are less important to you, and you spend more time on things that make you happy. Even though you may not see the impact of your investment right away, investing in yourself can greatly impact your life over time. As someone who comes from a family in which no one saw much need for improvement, and life was focused on merely surviving from one day to the other,

I can share *five* benefits of investing in yourself. First, investing in yourself will boost your confidence in your own abilities, and have a positive impact on your self-esteem. As well as giving you new knowledge and skills, focusing on your personal development will help you get to know yourself better. You will become more aware of your own unique set of strengths, values, and passions, and how you can use these to attain your goals.

Secondly, taking the time to invest in yourself will bring benefits to your career, both in the short and long term. You are your own greatest asset, and developing your skills can only boost your market value in the long run. Thirdly, anything you do to increase your worth as a person, be it aiming for a college degree, or signing up for a workshop, will help you grow your network and meet like-minded people. Over time, these relationships can turn into business opportunities or collaborations. That means keeping at the back of your mind that, as well as investing in yourself, you need to invest in your relationships. Networking is most successful when you approach it with a reciprocal mindset that sees benefits for you and for others, rather than just focusing on what's in it for you. Fourthly, knowledge is changing faster than ever before. Expanding and updating your skills will ensure that you are ready to adapt to these changes. Embracing lifelong learning will help you achieve a growth mindset, and to build the resilience needed to navigate life's inevitable challenges and adversities. Finally, continuous learning will lower your risk of mental health problems. That is because the mental stimulation provided by challenging yourself to learn new skills can help limit the adverse effects of aging on memory and mind.

You Are a Proven Blueprint for Success

Proven. Proof. Prove. These three words seem to define how I have spent the greater part of my life. For most of my life, I seem to have had this impulse to *prove* who I am. I have labored under the burden of providing *proof* that I am worthy. I have tortured myself trying to *prove* that I have value. I have bent over backward to accommodate mistreatment, all in an attempt to *prove* that I belong. What I didn't know was that I was already my own *proven* blueprint for success. What I didn't quite realize was that *Arletta the brand, Arletta the change agent,* and *Arletta the overcomer;* were already creating a blueprint that would inspire others to want to be better versions of themselves.

A blueprint is a guide for making something. It is a design or pattern that can be followed. The literal meaning of a blueprint is a piece of blue paper with plans for a building printed on it. Whenever we get ready to build something, we will need a blueprint. A blueprint is a simple drawing that outlines the particulars of a project design, from start to finish. If we were talking about building a home, or a restaurant, for instance, we would require a blueprint. When I was aspiring to open the first soul food restaurant in my community, the blueprint itself was my business plan. Included in that business plan were details about the location, the design or layout of the building, the menu, the staff, the daily operations, recipes, inventory, tools, and the certifications I would need to make it a successful venture. All these components need to be carefully laid out and executed for the restaurant business to even take off, and eventually succeed.

By a similar token, when it comes to our lives, we all have a blueprint for achieving success. Whether or not we actually activate that blueprint and its plan remains a matter of personal choice. With the wisdom of hindsight, I believe my major problem was that I didn't have sufficiently credible templates to use as examples for which direction my life ought to take. That was hardly surprising. There were so many broken pieces in my family history, and in my own story that, whenever I attempted to draw a path from where I was to where I wanted to be, the only guide I could rely on was my imagination and my hope. I had no proper example of what success should look like. We were so poor that we always had just enough to get by, and never an abundance of anything. Even as a little girl, I somehow aspired to change the world. While I wasn't quite sure how to achieve that, I just knew the desire was there, and it would continue to manifest as those small, ripple effects throughout my life.

Only recently, a childhood friend reached out to me to remind me of how I blessed her immensely when we were children. As I now recall, seeing myself as an outcast, I generally gravitated toward those who shared that view of themselves. In the classroom, I had taken notice of a girl no one appeared to want to sit with because of her poor personal hygiene, possibly caused by extreme poverty. I took it upon myself to sit with her, just so that she wouldn't feel so alone. I knew only too well what it felt like not to have a sense of belonging, and to feel like an outcast. When you are familiar with that sort of pain, you don't wish it upon anyone else. What finally placed me on the path to laying out my own blueprint was my recognition of myself, not as a part of my surroundings, environment, or culture, but by believing God's description of me. I am made in God's image. I am a great success because of my access to the kingdom, and my privileged position in it. I am a princess; a king's kid, as I'm fond of saying. Although I spent much of my life believing I didn't belong anywhere, in the deepest recesses of my heart, I truly believed that God was not guilty of any mistake when he created me. I refused to allow my environment to define the blueprint of success for my life. I drew inspiration from those who had gone before me to succeed. I resolved to develop a preparedness for my future, knowing only too well that there would be glorious opportunities presented to me that was not necessarily given to my mother and father, or even my grandparents or great grandparents, for that matter. I sought to create my own blueprint for success by relying on the ideologies and struggles of my forefathers and ancestors, in the hope of making a difference in my world, simply by doing my own part and contributing my own quota. I remain committed to discovering my own value in the vast marketplace of life, and those gifts that are unique to me, so that I can better serve others around me. In creating my very own blueprint for success, I have employed diligent stewardship, selflessness, and love to serve those that have been assigned to me to make a meaningful impact in their lives. Ultimately, it is my sincere belief that love leads the way, lights the path, and conquers all. Truly, that is the only blueprint I know, and will ever know.

Evaluate Yourself

The only way to improve on your own *thoughts* and *deeds* is to be completely honest about what you discover about yourself, no matter how ugly and unappealing it might seem. I call it *intellectual honesty.* Thorough self-evaluation demands that you critically analyze your own accomplishments, struggles, and goals. You will need to ask yourself critical questions like, *"What do I want to accomplish in my life? Do I have the confidence to believe that I can accomplish my goals? What type of energy am I putting out? What attitude am I deploying towards creating the life I desire?"* Have you ever heard the quote, *"Your energy introduces you long before you enter the room?"* In other words, people can feel your vibrations, and it is either they will gravitate toward you, or they will stay as far away from you as they possibly can. When it comes to me evaluating myself and my growth, I like to start with a list of goals, from which I proceed to my list of accomplishments, and end up with an honest and critical assessment of what needs improvement. I always ensure that this process is a frank and brutal self-analysis, and one in which there is simply no room for leniency. That is because I truly want to be the very best version of myself, and I am totally unwilling to leave the responsibility for my growth to others. Yet, I do not discount any clear evidence of my growth, and each day, I make it a point to look at where I am, and where I hope to be in the next few years. I set both long-term goals and short-term goals. Five years from now, I see myself as having achieved financial independence, without the need to ever struggle financially again. I see myself in my own dream home and one that is both self-designed and self-built. I have all the details already outlined in my head, and in my heart. At this point, I am no longer thinking with my head and feeling with my head. It is the other way around. I am now thinking with my heart and feeling with my head. That is the only thing that can make it a surreally emotional journey for me. I plan to be a New York Times Best Seller author, and be counted amongst the top twenty female speakers globally. My coaching business would have evolved to the status of a coaching firm that helps others to cut the learning curve in the time it takes to heal from the trauma that has caused deep wounds in their lives, so that they can now start operating at full capacity, and living their lives at the highest potential possible.

Invest in Your Education

The journey to achieving my educational goals was by no means a cakewalk. I did what everybody else coming from a background of poverty does to be able to earn their college degrees. I got into further debt by taking out student loans, and those loans came with compounded interest. Today, I still owe $45,000 in student loans. Day in, and day out, I worked extremely hard, standing on my feet for hours on end, in fast food restaurants, working as a bank teller, and as a medical support specialist. Despite all these, I still did not make sufficient money to cover my educational expenses. That did not stop me. I persevered. I simply kept applying for student loans, credit cards, and personal loans. I incurred one debt after the other. When I finally graduated, my elation was such that I went into a week-long binge of celebration, after which all the money I owed became my reality, and remains so. *Was it all worth it?* I'm not so sure. However, it is clear that my experiences are paving a much better path for me in life than even my education itself. Also, I know that my children felt the impact of every decision I took, and every sacrifice I made to survive during those years.

During my entire educational journey, I lived on food stamps, and although I worked full-time, I still couldn't afford to put myself through school. Coming from a background of grinding poverty, my struggle was real. My children and I basically lived on Kellogg's frosted flakes and maruchan ramen noodles to survive. Although I could not afford much, my children were always well-fed. These were the sacrifices I had to make to eventually earn credibility in my own market niche. My dreams were so big, and I desired so much to inch my way toward my platform. I had no one in my immediate vicinity to model my efforts after. My role model was Oprah Winfrey. I would often look at her and her story, and continually remind myself that the story always changes for the better later. I will admit that, quite often, I feel discouraged. The older I get, with my dreams still not manifesting, even though I am exerting all the effort prescribed by those I look up to in the industry, and whose path I so faithfully mirror, the more I sometimes feel a certain sense of futility. I often wonder when my time will come. When will I finally make it to the place of my dreams? I have sacrificed so much, and now, it seems I have nothing left to offer. Yet, my faith remains that God will beam His special grace upon me, and open up the way to my destiny. I believe it will happen. My only hope is that it will be while I still have a bit of my youth remaining.

Fail Your Way to Success

I will quote Les Brown. *"Give yourself another chance to make your dream a reality. Don't allow the delay to become a denial. Raise the bar on yourself. Increase your determination and explode your drive. You will fail on your way to success. Everything you experience can be used to grow through...not just to go through. Make your dream happen! You deserve it!"* My interpretation of these words by Mr. Brown is that, believe it or not, you must experience failure to truly appreciate success, and enjoy the benefits of that success. It might sound like a cliché, but failing your way to success is my way of saying that each time you fail, you actually get closer to your goal. Although you could have taken a more scenic route, the point remains that you will eventually arrive at your beautiful destination. It is true that each failure actually brings you closer to your goal. After all, failure serves as valuable feedback for a better course of action next time, thereby hastening your progress toward your goal. That is why your failures are the real source of your power. Your failures are the price you have to pay for your future success. Look at it this way. Each day is a new beginning for the rest of your life. Simply erase the memory of your past disappointments and the sadness that they caused. Yet, insist on retaining the lessons you learned from them, remembering that every experience is meant to teach you something.

I have my own definition of success, and of failure. What many consider failure, I simply do not consider failure. I tend to view my circumstance from a different lens. I believe that everyone can define success on their own terms. For instance, being a teenage mother is generally considered a failure. I will never forget my doctor at Sharpe Clinic in Fond du Lac, Wisconsin. Quite advanced in age, he would always threaten me with his machete each time I came on my prenatal visits. I was only sixteen. Waiting to see him was always a source of great anxiety. I always felt so much shame knowing that my son was conceived outside of wedlock. I was only a child myself, still learning what it meant to be mature. It was a classic case of a *baby mothering a baby.* That old white man would look me straight in my eyes and say, *"Let's hope you are the lucky one. Did you know one out of ten teenage girls who give birth die on the birthing table? Do you think this was a responsible choice? What do you think your chances of survival are?"*

That doctor was downright cruel. In stark reality, he traumatized me. A visit to his office always caused me to shut down, both mentally and emotionally. I believe this was the beginning of my journey of panic and anxiety disorder. I felt dirty and unworthy in his office. In the moments sitting in his office, I'd begin to strongly consider adoption. In the process of giving birth to my oldest son, Devan, he became stuck in my birth canal and lost 70% of his oxygen supply. The situation rather quickly escalated to an emergency cesarean section. In those tense moments before the operation, I recalled the

157

doctor's words. *"Let's hope you are the lucky one. Did you know one out of ten teenage girls who give birth die on the birthing table? Do you think this was a responsible choice? What do you think your chances of survival are?"* His words of doom had become my reality. I was facing death. I remember the entire episode, just as if it happened yesterday. It was a situation of total panic. It had quickly spiraled into an emergency, and with no time to allow the anesthesia to take effect, the cesarean incision was made in an effort to save my life and my baby's life.

To cut short a long story, the baby was born healthy, sound, and beautiful, with his eyes wide open, staring up at the sky. Seeing those big, beautiful eyes immediately convinced me that giving him up for adoption was simply not an option I was willing to pursue. As I went into recovery, the overnight separation from my son seemed like an eternity. After giving birth to my first son, it seemed I still wasn't a woman yet, because they took my baby the next time in a vaginal birth after a cesarean (VBAC). Even at that, I felt quite successful in giving birth the second time around. I share this story about the birth of my sons to make reference to the old wives' tale that if a woman does not give birth vaginally, she has not successfully given birth. Nothing could be further from the truth. Look at it this way. As long as you reach the finish line, it does not matter the route you took to get there. What matters is that you reached the finish line.

Success and failure look different to each person. At college, I failed twice before actually completing the journey to term. I had taken the scenic route, doing what I felt was best for me and my sons at the time. Trying to juggle the roles of student, wife, and mother simply proved too demanding for me. I dropped out during a difficult pregnancy, and I dropped out after I had my last son, to give him time to grow older. It was after all these that I returned to college to complete my studies. I did not successfully graduate from college until 2017, after a journey that began in 2003. Although I took the scenic route, I finally met my goal, and eventually failed my way to success. Investing time in my sons at such a critical time in their lives, and being a proper mother to them, was my focus, and my goal at that time. It was my way of investing in myself. Everything I do today, I do for those ten eyeballs staring back at me. My sons will always remain my *why*. I don't regret the scenic route. They were worth it. I am worth it. When all is said and done, I have learned how to fail successfully. I now see failure, not as an adversary, but as a friend.

Examine Your Circle

I can never stress enough just how important it is for you to have like-minded individuals with you on the road to success. Investing in yourself also means being careful about those with whom you relate. I have always been a loner. Yet, I have also grown to know the difference between *associates* and *friends*. So many people attach themselves to me with ulterior motives. I have learned that it is not everyone who craves a connection with you that has good intentions toward you. As a married woman, being a great cook and host, I would often have couples over for dinner. Sometimes, we would go out on dinner dates with such couples. I soon learned that some of the couples seemed to favor my husband over me. In fact, some of such so-called friends often aided and abetted my husband's infidelity behind my back. When my husband would leave me, they would often offer that he come to live with them, and he could bring anyone into their home as long as he helped maintain their home, since he was skilled at just about everything. In short, they capitalized on our marital problems.

159

It was quite tough for me to discover that not everyone means well to you. This travesty continued for a number of years during our marriage. Each time we quarreled, my husband would move in with them, purely as a decoy to engage in his extramarital affair with another single, vulnerable, and naive woman that needed whatever he had to offer at that time. It was a rather sickening cycle.

On the road to success, it is vital that the people around you are those who share your vision. They should also be trustworthy and loyal. You must set some sort of boundaries, otherwise, you will leave yourself open to betrayal and disappointment. I have quite a few associates and mentors, but none that I really consider friends, except my siblings. My family is my friends, and they are the people I prefer to keep with me on my success journey because I know they have my *front, back,* and *sides.*

Sometimes, when I speak with my sisters, it's almost as if they are more invested in my dreams and goals than me. Those are the type of people you want to keep around you. Those are the people that will help you to succeed. They will keep you moving forward whenever you want to throw in the towel. My sisters, especially, share hard truths with me that I need to hear, so that I do not wallow in self-pity. They constantly remind me of what I am capable of accomplishing. I appreciate them for simply being themselves; loyal and loving. Whether I win or lose, they remain with me, since our relationship is not based on what they can get from me, but rather on our mutual understanding of what true love means. My sister, Belinda, currently working on her master's degree in business, is an everyday source of inspiration. Coming from the background of a household in which there were never any discussions about education and self-improvement, Belinda is a prime example of strength, resilience, and perseverance. Blessed with uncommon beauty, grace, and style, she remains the main reason why I'm still chasing my own destiny, simply because she didn't choose to give up on *me* when I wanted to give up on *me*. She reached deep into her own resources of strength, lifted me, encouraged me, and held me until I was strong enough to carry on. My story illustrates just how important it is to choose wisely those whom you keep around you. In your struggle to defy the odds, these critical decisions can make or break you. Without my family, I would have failed a long time ago, and I remain grateful to each one of them for believing in me, building me up, and providing a safe space for me to hide whenever necessary.

Chapter 9
Reach for Your Goals

"Your ability to discipline yourself to set clear goals, and then to work toward them every day, will do more to guarantee your success than any other single factor."

- Brian Tracy

You probably have a vision of how you would like your life to be. Maybe you want to have a happy family, start your own business, eat healthier, be financially independent, or travel the world. Goal setting is important because it provides the steps you need to reach your goals. Especially when you have big goals, and there is no reason on Earth why you shouldn't dream big, the goal-setting process gives you a road map so you are headed in the right direction, and know the individual and specific steps you should take to make things happen. Setting goals gives you greater focus.

It provides you with an action plan you can review daily to make reaching goals part of your everyday schedule, instead of being merely something you will do "someday." Goal setting helps you manage your time better. Instead of feeling like you are always too busy to give proper attention to your goals, you will find that setting goals helps you use your time more wisely. More important things get done, and distracting or less important things are no longer that appealing. When you set goals, it is easier to stay motivated and inspired. You will find yourself gradually slipping into the habit of evaluating your goals before you sleep at night, and thinking about them as soon as you awaken in the morning. Achieving your goals becomes a way of life, and it gives you direction and purpose.

Identifying your life goals helps you make better decisions and gain more control over your future. When your goals are your priority, you will make decisions that align with your goals, and you will avoid anything and anyone that will waste your time.

Commit to Big and Worthy Goals

I have always been a big dreamer. This, in part, is because I lived in a nightmare. In other words, I was coming from a place of proficient practice. Virtually all of the time, the best, and maybe, the only way for me to escape the reality of being hungry; being uncomfortable, and hot; being continually in a state of lack, or wondering when the next brutal punishment or beating from my father would occur, was to slip into daydreaming, and imagine being somewhere else; anywhere else. I would spend hours on end daydreaming, and thinking about what life might have been, or could alternatively be. Television was the soothing balm that offered and added much-needed color to my fantasies. Television was an important part of my growing-up years. I spent endless hours watching sitcoms like *Family Matters, Full House, The Cosby Show, and It's a Different World.* They led me into the world of make-believe. They also ingrained in me the belief that there was so much more this big, wide world could offer me. I knew I wasn't going to remain young forever. My mind went riot with the imagination of being happily married to someone who wouldn't hurt me the way my father hurt my mother. I wallowed in the imagination of being a princess pursuing a brilliant career. Yes, a princess with golden slippers and a shimmering ball gown. I saw myself as a rich, beautiful princess who ate ice cream all day long and sailed to the park on a handsome pony, as often as it pleased me. In my mind's eye, I hadn't the least worry about being told what I could, and couldn't do.

Little did I know that I was actually living in ignorance of the ugly state of affairs, both at home and outside the home. I didn't know that my mother was trying all she could to protect and shield me from the stark ugliness of the world outside of the walls of our small apartment. The streets were filled with drug dealers and crackheads. The sidewalks were infested by alcoholics, prostitutes, and *Chester The Molester,* the comic archetype of the man whose preoccupation was the sexual molestation of women and young girls. As depicted in the famous comic strip of the same name, *Chester The Molester* was that dirty old man who liked to prey on little girls, taking their innocence through demeaning sexual acts, raping and exploiting them, all the while remaining anonymous, and swearing them to secrecy. We all have someone like that in our families. Everyone knows they are there, but no one likes to speak about them. Many families house deep, dark secrets of Chester The Molesters, who hide under the title of *dad, uncle, cousin,* and even *brother.* The mere thought of that brings me to tears, as I think of all the trauma and pain that exists in the hearts and minds of so many of the women in my family that I love so much. So much damage was done to those women, and many of the perpetrators of that damage have long been buried years ago. Yet, we still carry the emotional scars associated with those experiences. Sadly, but truthfully, the damage they caused will continue to outlive them in totality.

It is difficult to be a *big dreamer* when everything around you seems so dark and gloomy. Fortunately for me, I seem to have come into this world with an extraordinarily fertile imagination, and a big mind. As I got older, I held onto my dreams and my goals, all in an effort to help me surmount the many obstacles I would encounter. I learned early enough to always *see it before I see it.* Setting goals for myself was the way to get me as close as possible to what I imagined to be the very best version of myself. Naturally, such goals were almost invariably about my appearance, weight, finances, education, and love life. Most of the big goals I set for myself were always in those categories. For instance, my weight has always been something that I repeatedly set goals for. I struggle with my weight all the time. Even though I am only too aware that diabetes runs in my family history, and that it is a dangerous and deadly disease, I lack sufficient self-control, willpower, and discipline to adhere to any diet that places even minimal restrictions on my eating habits. I have been obese for the greater part of my life. The highest weight I ever attained was 255 pounds, while the lowest weight of my adult life has been 212 pounds. Try as much as I have, I cannot seem to attain the 160 pounds that are supposed to be my healthy weight goal. Thankfully, I have no challenges with my blood pressure and cholesterol level. Because I am what is called *big-boned,* I tend to carry my weight well, and in a manageably proportioned way. Yet, my weight goal remains one that continues to elude me.

In contrast, I set the goal to become the first individual in my family to become truly educated. That was a huge goal that I became determined to achieve after becoming a high school dropout. I attended Moraine Park Technical College to obtain my High School Equivalency Diploma after becoming pregnant with my first son at the age of sixteen. I missed a lot of school hours because of a difficult pregnancy. However, I was determined to finish school, having witnessed my mother's own struggle to get her GED while we were living at the homeless shelter. My mother did it. She finished school as a homeless single mom, caring for her children all on her own. I

166

always say my mother is my *why*, if only because she is a repository of all the attributes and strengths that I aspire to.

I set another goal for myself after the birth of my fourth and final son, Josiah. I decided I would go back to college, complete my studies, and earn my degree. I had previously dropped out twice. After this, I set a goal to become the first person of color in history to serve as a council person in the city of Fond du lac. I achieved it. Then, I set a goal to be the first person in my family to start a viable business and work for herself. I achieved that too, and more. I have established three businesses since setting that goal. I set a goal to, someday, author a book that would tell my story. The book you hold in your hands is the eloquent manifestation of that desire and the attainment of that goal. As you read this story of me making the transition from *trauma to triumph,* and *defying the odds* from every angle, I urge you to recognize that *what became possible for me was in part because I believed in what was possible for me.* I also understood that any goal one sets for oneself demands work. A goal without the corresponding work it demands is a mere idea. A goal without a plan, or a strategy to achieve it, is merely an idea. I set big goals because I am a big dreamer, and I believe all things are possible if you dare to believe them. I don't believe in glass ceilings. I believe we only have the limitations we set for ourselves, and even those limitations are not set in concrete, because what God has designed for each one of us belongs to us, and there is no way to get around that.

Prioritize Your Goals

The reason why it has been so difficult for me to achieve some goals, yet not quite as difficult to achieve others, is simply because of where each goal ranks on my scale of priority. We tend to make time and room for those things that are most important to us. Every other consideration is a mere excuse. The principal reason why I have failed to achieve set goals to lose weight on so many occasions is that my desire to eat my sweets far outstripped my desire to see myself wearing a thinner waistline. Was I upset by that personal weakness? Yes, I was. The conflict between a craving for my sweets, and my desire for a more attractive waistline was a real and disconcerting one. In the final analysis, I wanted to eat my cake and have it. Unfortunately for me, matters do not quite work that way. The only path to achieving the goals we set for ourselves is to be disciplined, focused, and unflinching in our firm resolve. Our goals must be prioritized for us to accomplish them.

For instance, the goal I set to go back to school to obtain my high school diploma, after dropping out due to teenage pregnancy, most certainly could not have been attainable had I not prioritized the goal. There were so many excuses I could have made at that time, including, a diploma wasn't such a priority anyway, the baby was too young, I had to work to earn a living, I had no help, and who would babysit for me, I don't really understand the course curriculum anyway, I didn't have the time to study, and a host of other feeble excuses. Thankfully, it did seem as if I hungered for something different. After the birth of my son, the life I led prior to that no longer held any sustainable attractions for me. At that time, my sole preoccupation was my son, Devan. His needs totally overrode anything else I considered of any importance concerning me. I simply wanted a better life for him, and the only guaranteed path to that better life was an education. I needed to go back to school and earn a diploma that would earn me a better-paying job, especially since his father had bluntly refused to claim him as his son. Clearly, I was up the creek without a paddle. If that was not enough to ginger me to the extraordinary effort, nothing would. My son needed me to prioritize what was more important so that he could have an even brighter future than the one I was painting for myself.

Execution Over Excuses

Thomas A. Edison, the great inventor, and industrialist, once wrote, *"Having a vision for what you want is not enough. Vision without execution is hallucination."* He was right. How badly do you want that which you desire? What are you willing to sacrifice to get you to the mark? What are you willing to do? I have often heard it said that faith without works is dead. The same holds true for goals. Goals without execution will only remain that; goals. They will never come to pass. Goals can only be achieved when a strategy is employed, and that strategy must be implemented in the form of actions that are executed to get you there. The goal that I set to become the first black woman in history to serve on the city council of my community was not attained with ease. That Herculean feat was achieved only because of a well-executed campaign, and a strategy. I had to become so visible that the voters became aware of my vision and goals regarding the community I was to serve. I made it clear that I was there to be a voice for the underserved and underrepresented in our community. I propagated the message, which was quite true, that our community lacked *equity, inclusion,* and *diversity.*

Those who had migrated from other states and communities did not feel welcome in our community because there was no one in a position of power that *looked like them.* It's hard to see yourself as a success story when you don't see success in those with whom you can easily relate. I perfectly understood this sentiment because of my own personal frame of reference, and I desired to change that narrative for others. So, I set a goal. I put a plan in place and set out to discover what it would take to have a seat at the table and to discuss and offer a more diverse perspective on the decisions that were being taken that ultimately affected all of us as constituents. Frankly, if I had not achieved the goal of becoming the first college graduate in my family, my declaration to become an elected official would not have been taken seriously. In any case, I would have lacked sufficient knowledge, credibility, and exposure to operate in that realm.

Local government administration and procedure is a different ball game altogether. I endured each day feeling as if I didn't belong. It was one thing running for the office of councilperson. It was an entirely different challenge being in that legislative chamber and trying to carry out the duties of a councilperson. It was a very tough undertaking, and I can't recall a single day when I did not want to throw in the towel, and resign. In any case, I had more than adequate help in that regard, as I received so many threatening emails and phone calls demanding that I resign. The prejudiced and racist people within our community made it abundantly clear that they didn't want me sitting in their legislative chambers, nor did they want my *blackness* staining their righteous White supremacist legacy. Yet, I was lawfully and duty elected to the position. Within me, I was in familiar territory. Wanting to quit had always been my usual recourse whenever I was on the threshold of accomplishing something great. I genuinely believed that *if it didn't hurt much, it could not have been worth much.* The nagging urge to give up has always been a clear indication that I was onto something grand, or perhaps, epic if you will.

I have a surprise for you. I did not resign. To express matters more accurately, I simply refused to resign, no matter how mean my adversaries were to me and my children. I simply chose to *defy* all of them, no matter the odds they chose to stack against me. I *defied all odds* and remained in that legislative chamber. I *defied* all that was happening behind closed doors in my own home. My home front was a battlefield all on its own. I was a victim of domestic violence, and there was so much chaos around me, all of the time. My reality was really quite stark and ugly. I wasn't safe at my own home. wasn't safe in the chambers. In other words, I wasn't safe anywhere, sometimes not even from myself. Life was hard, and it was harrowing. Yet, I still chose *execution over excuses.* My children continued to remain mine *why*. I continued to press on towards my goals because I knew my sons were watching me and mimicking my every action. I did not want them to grow up believing that adversity was an excuse to give up. Adversity is, and will always be your opportunity to square up, and refusing to blink, continue to push through until you reach the goal you set out to accomplish. Giving up, in or out is never optional. Defeat is never an option. I set out to establish a *no-excuse* realm for my family, and my boys. With me and those boys, the keyword will always be *executed.* My philosophy was *executed over excuse.* I needed my boys to *see it and live by it* so that when life happened to them, as it inevitably would, at some point or the other, they would automatically see the adversity as an opportunity to grow, and evolve into better versions of themselves.

Act as If You Have Nothing to Lose

The truth is that when I set out to achieve my goals, I didn't have to act as if I had nothing to lose, since, indeed, I had nothing to lose. On the contrary, I had everything to gain. In any case, I was coming from a place of *nothing* and had become accustomed to dreaming about and reaching for what I believed was possible. Although I didn't have anyone with whom I could model how to obtain a college degree, I surrounded myself with those who did. Naturally, my imagination came in quite handy. Having a clear picture of the success you aspire to is very important. But, if that picture doesn't exist, you have the power to create it. I have learned along my journey that you can create the life you want by ensuring that your thoughts dwell upon only those things that are in alignment with that life. *In other words, to live the dream, you will have to dream about life.*

Having a growth mindset is important for achieving your goals. You must imagine yourself standing right in the place that everyone says you don't deserve to be. I do not dwell on what isn't working well. Rather, I fix my sight on what is. Then, I choose to do more of that. As I progressed through college, I never imagined the cost. I never calculated the cost of success. I simply plunged headlong into the journey. I saw it. I believed in it. I achieved it. I have a word of caution. By no means do I aim to casually dismiss the hurdles I had to surmount, nor do I mean to downplay the sacrifices I had to make. One thing I am absolutely clear about is that, as soon as you are sufficiently hungry, you will find the ways, and the means, to eat. I had nothing to lose, but everything to gain because I was already at *ground zero.* Every step forward was better than standing still. Every move was considered progress because it got me closer, and closer to my dream. I gave everything I had to achieve my education, in part because I believed that it was the key to unlocking the door to my next mansion of success. All my goals worked seamlessly together as a process, and not a single one existed in isolation from the others.

Engage in Self-Sacrifice to Delay Gratification

In order to have anything *new* you must be willing to give up something *old*. None of my goals came to fruition without some form of sacrifice. Sacrifice has become a common theme of my entire life journey. Self-sacrifice became an uncompromising mandate for me to achieve my goals. For instance, when I was raising my newborn son as a teenager, I forfeited the freedom of going out to hang out with friends. My mother made it clear that she would not give me room to bring another baby into her house. In other words, if she let me run around freely, leaving my son at home, the chances were high that I would be somewhere *laying down* to make another. My mother was so strict with me that I hated her for it at that time, yet I know it was all for my own good. She constantly pushed me to live by a higher standard and to be better. My mother never told me anything without offering a credible explanation, or a quote to validate her request of me, and I loved that about her.

When I was in college, striving to get an education, I lacked the time and the finances to do as I wished, and that included adequate rest or sleep. I would repeatedly give up my rest to work and provide for my children, and do my homework to maintain good grades throughout my college career. Naturally, it was very difficult for me to have any type of social life while working to earn a living, and doing homework to maintain good grades. My marriage was also a victim. Achieving a balance was extremely difficult, but that is the sacrifice you have to make when reaching for your goals. My second former husband could never understand my sacrifices for schoolwork. He always murmured and complained that I always made time for class and work, but when it was time to perform my duties as a wife, I was always exhausted or asleep.

I did the very best I could under difficult circumstances, but something always went lacking because of my sacrifice to build a better life for us all.

When I was working toward becoming a councilperson, the sacrifice I had to make was in my private life. I was subjected to so much exploitation and embarrassment, as the media constantly attacked and targeted my family for political reasons. I lost friends because of my political viewpoints, especially because I am a republican and not a Democrat. I lost valuable friendships because I spoke out against a racist couple in our community. While everyone else did not take on the fight, for me it became a personal crusade because they were attacking people who looked like me. The George Floyd episode in Minnesota was a turning point for race relations all over the nation, and there were silent protests all over the country. I participated in quite a few such protests locally, and was basically vilified for my views on that too. I believe we have all been given a voice, and that it is our obligation to use that voice in a way that can either build up our community, or tear it down. I choose to create a positive impact even in the face of sacrifice that is seemingly too costly. I believe in standing up for what is right. My mother taught me the tenacity, and the sheer grit that I have today. I refuse to stand down when I am passionate about a subject of any kind. I will stand until change comes, just like my forefathers did because I believe in worthy sacrifice to achieve equity. I believe in giving up what is necessary to make a difference, or to meet my goals.

One of the highest points of my life journey will always be the restaurant that I once owned, *A Family Affair Soulfood Kitchen.* Sacrifice will never be a sufficiently expressive word to describe all that I gave up to see that dream become a reality. Because I lost everything I put into that business venture as a sacrifice, my final verdict is simply that you should be willing to *go big or go home*. I sank all that I had into that restaurant because I believed in it one hundred percent. Not only did I believe in the dream, but I also believed in creating generational wealth for my sons. I believed in my ability to create culinary dishes that were true to my ancestry, and to my bloodline. My principal motivation was to establish a legacy for my mother and her skills as an accomplished gourmet cook. This was borne of my willingness to pursue a goal and to sacrifice all that was necessary to create something that had never before been done in our family. It was a rare achievement that I remain proud of, and I am still in the process of healing from the loss of that beautiful enterprise, but I believe that I will yet rise like the phoenix from the ashes. I believe that God can and will use everything that I have endured to help me *defy the odds* in my life, and to forge ahead into the future He has planned for me. Therefore, I choose not to dwell on the sacrifice, because I recognize that its purpose is to get me that much closer to my destiny, and the ultimate calling God has for me.

Ultimately, that destiny will make up for all the nights I couldn't hang out, all the times I couldn't go to the movies, or hang out late, and all the times I couldn't buy my favorite things, all because I was trying to conserve funds for my tuition payment, or put gas in my car or food on the table. The sacrifice was worth it for the season God has called me into today. What would there be to share with you had I not endured all the turmoil that life has thrown my way? Who would I even be? I do know that my story is mine, your story is yours, and our combined stories are both relevant and worth sharing. In the final analysis, I am glad that you are here to walk through these pages with me, to discover all that has happened in my transition from trauma to triumph.

Chapter 10
Adopt An Attitude of Gratitude

"Gratitude is a powerful catalyst for happiness. It is the spark that lights a fire of joy in your soul."

- Amy Collette

There is no greater power on this Earth than pure, unconditional love. That is not surprising. In its highest nature, love is actually the Will of God. Most of us think that unconditional love relates only to love between human beings. Nothing could be further from the truth. Its real application is love for each and every situation you find yourself in, including those that are upsetting, or even extremely difficult. Naturally, it is also love for all the people you come in contact with, embracing them with open arms, like an innocent child. The only way we can demonstrate unconditional love for all things, and for all people, is if and when we are filled with gratitude for all that we experience, and for all that comes our way. That is why the greatest love of all is *gratitude*.

Gratitude speaks into the deepest core of your relationship with God.

Gratitude reveals the fullness of your life.

Gratitude transforms what you have into enough, with more to spare.

Gratitude turns rejection into acceptance.

Gratitude turns confusion into order.

Gratitude turns haziness into clarity.

Gratitude turns your simple meal into a feast.

Gratitude turns your house into a home.

Gratitude turns that total stranger into your friend.

Gratitude reveals the beauty of your past.

Gratitude brings a sense of peace into your today.

Gratitude creates a brilliant vision for your tomorrow.

Gratitude spices up your menu for a truly delicious life.

Be a Love Finder, Not a Fault Finder

It is my belief that any suggestion that one should be a love finder already insinuates that, at some point, love itself was lost. There have been several instances in my life in which I recall feeling as if I needed to *trade out*, or suppress, so to speak, how I genuinely felt about a situation, just so I could overlook the shortcomings of others. There is no doubt that I have ended up receiving the short end of the stick, especially in my judgment of the *seasonal* people in my life, and the *lifetime* players in my life. I hasten to add here that, for the *lifetime* players, I mostly attempted to force them to remain so. For several reasons, more often than not, associated with childhood trauma, I have found it incredibly difficult to release those relationships in my life that no longer serve my best purpose. I tended to hold on for dear life in the misguided belief that in the process, I could avoid the trauma of abandonment all over again. I have a rather important question for you. *"How many times have you tried to hold on to someone, or to something, that it seemed all but clear that God Himself was trying to free you from?"* The rejection I felt as a child, and its wound were so deep that even the thought of someone walking away from me triggers overwhelming anxiety to this day. I have taken every possible step to remedy this persistent feeling, but as we will all admit, some days will still remain better than others. Learning to see the good in every situation, and in everyone, is a very difficult feat to achieve. Over the years, however, I have truly recognized my own choice and power of either choosing *love* or choosing to a *fault*. I recognize, also, that pointing fingers does not resolve conflicts. In fact, as I have dis, pointing fingers and finding fault does nothing more than lead to even greater conflict, frustration, and distress. Difficult situations will always call for difficult decisions. As someone who has suffered so much trauma, and consistently doing the work to transition from trauma to triumph, I have discovered that, for my own well-being, and my peace of mind, it is far better not to hold onto the negative energy generated by those who don't seem to understand the effects of their own unfortunate choices on me. Yet, I also realize that, possibly, they are well aware of the effect of their negativity on me, but care more for their own self-preservation than they care about mine. Perhaps it is my own empathetic nature that seems to draw narcissistic persons to me. Perhaps it is God who wants me to learn lessons from such encounters. The latter is probably closer to my truth.

As the Bible relates, once, the Israelites, while in the wilderness, went around the same mountain over and again, until they were instructed, *"You have compassed this mountain long enough, go ye northward!"* I often wonder if God is not musing to Himself, *"Arletta, I see that you are just not getting the lesson here. So, I will bring the experience to a close for you."* My mother would always tell me that I wore rose-colored glasses. In other words, I always seemed to find the beauty in even the ugliest of things. In the final analysis, that is what probably qualifies me as a *love finder,* rather than a *fault finder.* At some point, I actually resented God for giving me a heart of compassion and empathy. The reason is simple. Those traits have exposed me to exploitation far too often. I have been taken advantage of many more times than I care to remember. I resented God for a naïve character flaw that seemed to prevent me from recognizing evil motives in others. Why did men who desired an intimate relationship with me seek to hurt me, use me, abuse me and eventually abandon me?

My former husband struggled with many conflicts and failings. He was older than me by fourteen years, because of which I labored to understand the illusion that, being more mature, he would have acquired a certain understanding of the real issues of life. I was grossly mistaken. While he might have been mature in age, he was far less mature in prudence and judgment. He struggled with being loyal, honest, and a provider. For years, the burden of our upkeep rested solely on me. All he did was spend his money to purchase the marijuana that kept him on a perpetual *high.* I constantly struggled, on my own, to ensure that all our necessities were met. Despite that, I took this as an opportunity to look beyond his faults, and try to find ways to demonstrate to him those contrasting attributes that would be more helpful to our marriage. I demonstrated loyalty and love, even though they were not reciprocated. I tolerated and accommodated him, constantly making allowances and excuses for him, because, deep down inside of me, I dreaded the possibility of losing him. I did not want to feel the pain of watching someone else walk away from me. I put up with deep emotional, mental, and physical abuse and trauma, for over fourteen years. I justified his appalling behavior for years, until I finally discovered that I needed to give myself the same compassion I was giving him, which he did not, and could not, appreciate.

I gradually grew into the truth that, being a love finder, and not a fault finder, was also a manifestation of gratitude. My self-love meant being willing to hold myself to standards that were not defined by the fact that others chose to hurt me. It meant screaming at the top of my lungs, *"I am not defined by what I have endured!"* It was time for me to be grateful for all that God had provided, and all that God had permitted me to endure through faith, fortitude, and perseverance. It wasn't until I stopped finding fault in *myself* and chose to love *myself*, that my own truth began to positively impact others. If all we can see is how difficult a situation is, we will never be able to see the good in that situation, such that we can feel gratitude for the lessons contained in it, and learn from them.

Take Nothing and No One for Granted

Cynthia Ozick wrote, *"We often take for granted the very things that most deserve our gratitude."* She is right. I know this to be a truth of my own experience, if only because I am employing the opportunity afforded by writing these words to reflect, and write from a place of integrity and honesty. I can sincerely recall times in which I have taken people for granted in my life. I believe in the principle of reaping and sowing. I believe that although I may not have intended for my actions to have an adverse effect on others on those occasions, I still suffered the consequences. There were times when I could not provide for my children and myself, as a single mother. Need I add the abusive relationships I had to endure while being consistently immersed in a *fight or flight* mode? For me, it was a landscape of constantly seeking to survive, never at rest, never feeling stable, and always on the alert as to what could go wrong at an unguarded moment, and which, almost invariably, did go wrong most of the time.

In my life's journey, I have found that certain people seem to have been assigned to *watch* over me. I prefer to call them the *angels* of my life. For instance, whilst attending junior high school, the school principal was a man named Kelly Noble. The man demonstrated rare kindness and compassion towards me, and an uncommon understanding of the marginalization my family was experiencing. Mr. Noble would often summon me to his office, just to ask about my welfare, and conditions at my home front. Naturally, he was only too aware that I grew up in a single-parent, poverty-stricken household. Mr. Noble made it his business to know how his students were faring, especially after school hours. My mother was subsisting on *welfare*, and she budgeted strictly such that we could live on $600 a month, one month after the other. My mother would give each one of us $20 as a monthly allowance. I would spend $16 on a bus pass, and I would have $4 remaining to get an extra milkshake, slice of pizza, or go to Taco John's around the corner, and get fried potato rounds. We called them "potato oles." This particular treat was the highlight of the month for me. Anyhow, Mr. Noble would check on me, and every now and again, he would send me home with some money for my mother. If he knew I wished to participate in an extra-curricular activity at school, he would often take care of the fee. He never wanted me to feel marginalized, and because of his generosity, I never did.

I recall that after I made the cheerleading squad, Mr. Noble found out that all the girls bought the same pair of shoes, but because I couldn't afford those shoes, I wore the only pair I had. Mr. Noble gave me money to buy those pairs of Nike shoes. Those shoes were a young girl's delight. They had interchangeable colors in the *swoosh*, to match our cheerleading uniform. My heart smiles with gratitude whenever I recall all those people in our lives whom we should never take for granted. Although it was clear that Mr. Noble harbored only the best intentions and outcomes for me, my *sense of gratitude* soon dissolved into a *sense of entitlement.* Soon enough, I began to trouble him, almost begging him, for little things that were remarkable only in their insignificance. Sadly, I started to take Mr. Noble for granted. I would ask for $3 for extra lunch. I would request $5 to go to school dances. I would ask for help with additional food items, even after my mom had received her food stamps. Needless to say, I had slipped into the extremely bad habit of taking Mr. Noble's kindness for granted. I am not proud of that scorecard, I can assure you. If you have people in your life that genuinely love you, and want the best for you, refuse to take them for granted. As a child, I interpreted my attitude as a survival strategy. As an adult, I recognize that I was in the early stages of manipulation to get what I wanted by using my family's misfortune as leverage to get what I wanted. It was wrong. The only way we can truly and sustainably remain grateful for what others do for us is if we refuse to take them for granted. As soon as we take others for granted, we lose all respect for them, and as soon as we lose respect for them, we cannot feel a sense of gratitude towards them.

Our experiences deserve the same orientation. As soon as we take our experiences for granted, we cannot be grateful for the lessons they teach us. Mr. Noble taught me, in my youth, that there are good, wholesome people in the world, regardless of race or background. He taught me that there are people in the world who are full of compassion and love. Because of Mr. Noble, and those other people who were angels in my life, I spend each and every day acknowledging those that I am grateful for, and this has now become, rather than the occasional, mere reflection, but an enduring lifestyle.

Discarding the Habit of Complaining

Life is like a game of cards that are already scheduled, leaving you absolutely no choice in the matter of whether or not to play in it. You must play in it. You might as well play to win. You have to negotiate with life to get the best out of life. It is up to us to choose how to play the cards we are dealt. I believe the songwriter who wrote, *"You gotta know when to hold'em', know when to fold' em', know when to walk away, and know when to run!"* There was a time when the only way I knew to express my feelings was to complain until I realized matters could always be worse than they already are. It is true that life could always be worse. Complaining always seems the easy thing to do when we feel pressured. It is easier to *speak* what we feel instead of *speaking* what it is we would like to see. A life filled with despairing events taught me how to sulk in those negative feelings, and to feel sorry for myself, instead of choosing gratitude for what was already working in my life.

A few years ago, I began a gratitude practice to help me in my faith walk with God. There was always something circumstantial occurring in my life that I felt warranted my complaints, even though complaining rarely produced any good fruit. Complaining only amplified the circumstances. I recall, as a jobless mother, living in an apartment complex with all four of my children. I wasn't exactly sure how I was going to provide for those boys. However, I was a faithful servant of God, and I believed in going to church, and actively participating in church activities. I went to my pastor and told him that I had no job and that I had applied for a job at a gas station right down the street from my house. My oldest son, Devan, was old enough to watch over his siblings while I worked a flexible schedule. What this meant was that the time I would normally be at church would now be devoted to working. I told my pastor that I could no longer attend church on Sunday because I had to work. His response was, *"Isn't God bigger than your circumstances? You complain about not having what you need yet you don't trust God to provide."* He told me that I was behaving no better than the children of Israel who murmured and complained incessantly while in the wilderness. My pastor didn't believe it was God's will that I take on that job, and not be able to attend church. So, I declined the job. Barely a week later, I was offered a job as a bank teller at US Bank by the bank's president, Mrs. Claudia Vopal. She invited me to visit with my pastor, and offered me a job on the spot. God provided a new job opportunity that paid more and left my Sundays free for church attendance. I chose to have faith, and not take what was offered out of desperation. I chose to trust God, no matter my circumstances.

I recall when my son, Moniteque, was suffering from mental and behavioral disorders. The distressing diagnosis was intermittent borderline explosive disorder, impulse disorder, and transitional disorder. I would complain all the time about having to leave my job to come to school to relieve the staff because of my son's disorder. Raising a blue rose is never easy. I call my son a blue rose because of how special and unique he is. He is a blue rose because God trusts only a few of us with them. Our path was an extremely difficult one. It is not easy raising a child with disabilities and being a single mother dealing with domestic abuse and poverty all at the same time. Life simply wasn't easy. I complained the whole way through.

Yet, God still granted me the grace to raise my son through every up and down, until he became of age and independent. Moniteque now lives on his own, living an incredibly productive life as a young man. Unknown to me, the entire time I was complaining, God was only honoring me with a gift. It is important that we carefully assess what we consider stressful. At such times, it is often only God's grace and love toward us that is carrying us, and we should be grateful for that. I needed to address my attitude of complaining and finally recognized it as a tendency to see only what is lacking in my life. Complaining simply means we are focused on lack, and not on what we do have to be thankful for.

Practice Humility

Gordon B. Hinckley wrote, *"Being humble means recognizing that we are not on earth to see how important we can become, but to see how much difference we can make in the lives of others."* He couldn't have put it better. There was a time in my life when I actually believed humility was a negative word. I rather simplistically interpreted humility to mean allowing others to walk all over you. For me, humility meant you were like a rug, in the sense that, when life deals you its difficult hand, you are content to just lie down there, and never fight back. Nothing could be further from the truth. I got it all wrong. Actually, humility requires strength and courage. Humility is being a royal personage without a crown. Far too often has humility been perceived in an improper context. Humility simply connotes setting aside your pride and staying very clear of arrogance.

To be humble means to recognize and acknowledge your own shortcomings, and to refuse to think too highly of yourself, rather valuing the feelings and sensibilities of others over yours. I have learned so many ways in which to practice humility, and they are not grandiose. They are simply easily applicable and practical strategies. For instance, choosing to allow others to speak, and listening to them without interruption is very ennobling. I will be the first to admit just how long it took for this practice to take root in me. That was not so surprising. I had always been someone who needed to fight to be heard. This came from years of being overlooked, with feelings that were never considered worthy of respect. It might also have come from being a middle child. I easily remained under the radar in our household, as there were so many of us.

Another form of humility is to ignore the negative actions of others, and rather, choose to be more optimistic. This all requires practice. I recall a day at choir rehearsal in which I learned a valuable lesson on humility. I will never forget it. I was in active rehearsal with fifteen other members. My pastor, who was also the musician, played a Hammond B3 organ. On an amusing note, if he gets to read this book, he would never forgive me, and might even consider it an act of sacrilege, if I failed to mention the type of organ he played. We were going over a song, and feeling I could not hit the high-octave soprano note, I exclaimed, *"I can't get this!"* He stopped the music abruptly. I will always remember the look on his face. If looks could kill, I would have dropped dead. The one word we were not allowed to utter during rehearsals was *"can't."* I remained very argumentative and went back and forth about what I believed to be my own limitations. Pastor Haywood told me to *"Humble yourself and stop being insubordinate and rude. Just listen and offer your best."* My response was one of total disservice to myself. I retorted, *"Maybe you should humble yourself!"* Needless to say, I wasn't around for very long.

I was asked to leave rehearsal, and because the person who gave me a ride to church was still in rehearsal, I had to sit on the front steps of the church, waiting for rehearsal to end. Soon, Pastor Haywood's wife, Pastor Beverly Haywood, came along and asked why I looked so pitiful and sad, and I burst into tears and told her what had happened. She helped me to see where my error had been and suggested an apology to get back to rehearsal. Although I took Pastor Beverly's advice, my feelings were terribly hurt by a practice of humility in which I was forced to admit I was wrong in speaking out of turn to my pastor. That shows just how tough the practice of humility can often be. Yet, like anything else that you do repetitively, the practice of humility will eventually become a part of the fabric of who you are, and it will become a natural response to adversity. As Criss Jami wrote, *"To share your weakness is to make yourself vulnerable; to make yourself vulnerable is to show your strength."* Sharing this story with you has humbled me even more. Only a humble heart can be grateful. A conceited and proud heart has a sense of entitlement, and cannot be grateful, even for the little things. The more humble we are, the more we can accept that nothing comes by our might, but by the might of God, and we can then be filled with gratitude to Him who is the beginner and the finisher of all things.

Open a Gratitude Journal

While I actually started keeping a gratitude journal many years ago, it was not until fairly recently that I became very intentional about keeping a daily journal of the things I am truly grateful for. This is because, possibly very much like you, I too have moments when I focus more on where I am lacking, and less on what God has already provided. I cannot sufficiently stress the importance of keeping a personal, guided journal that you can reference at any point to remind you of all the people, places, and things to be grateful for. I keep a simple journal of about 100 pages at my bedside. As soon as I rise in the mornings, after thanking God for the breath in my body, and the eyes with which to see, I quickly write down the date, and start the sentence, *"I am grateful for ...."*

Keeping a gratitude journal reminds me that no matter how difficult life may seem at times, there is always something to focus on outside of the turmoil. If that is the case, why shouldn't I choose the *good* over the *bad?* I recognize that there will always be people that possess more than I do, and those who possess far less, but the key is to be content with what I already have. My gratitude entry can, at times, be something very significant. Yet, on some days, it can be as simplistic as thanking God for my Keurig coffee machine and having K-pods and my favorite creamer to top it off. What I love most about my gratitude journal is that it is mine. It represents my personally expressed thoughts about what to focus on, and what to be truly grateful for. With each entry, I am reminded that there is always a bright spot on the horizon, no matter how painful the lingering trauma may be. I can seek out the silver lining, simply by turning back a page in my gratitude journal and reading the previous day's entry. Should you choose to keep a gratitude journal, as I recommend that you do, I can promise that you will discover joy in all things. This set routine of acknowledging, writing, and meditating on what you already have, and which you can be grateful for, lessens the impulse to focus on what you perceive as missing from your life. You will notice, after a few months, that your mindset has shifted, and you are now simply eager to express appreciation and humility to God for meeting all your needs.

This is the place I am longing to arrive at. It is a place of no worries, and I am well on my way there.

Chapter 11
Celebrate Your Successes

*"The more you praise and celebrate your life,
the more there is in life to celebrate."*

- Oprah Winfrey

As we gradually approach the end of our journey together, the more I realize that my life is a *party*, and I am the guest of honor! I am an empathetic person, so it is already an uphill task for me to push myself. Also, it is only natural and normal for me to nurture others, while it is a big struggle for me when it comes to showing myself the same empathy, care, and love that I give others. Yet, if the truth is told, I have so much to celebrate. My transition from *trauma to triumph* has not been an easy journey, and if only because of that, it demands and deserves celebration. I am u dear an obligation to celebrate myself for all those times I was told I would never amount to anything remarkable, and that I would never be anyone significant.

Let's face it, I ultimately had something to prove, not only to them but also to myself. Although I had self-limiting beliefs about celebrating my successes, I eventually learned that I didn't need to prolong the celebration because I was waiting on others to validate me. In other words, I needed no one's permission to celebrate myself. After all, who can be prouder of all my accomplishments than myself? I choose to self-celebrate the person that I have become. I choose to celebrate the woman that I am now. I am not celebrating the future *me,* because I haven't met *her* yet. However, I have no doubt whatsoever that she is fabulous, healthy, alive, and an inspiration to women all over the United States, and beyond. My life is rich in those glorious *moments* that deserve celebration. It is rightly said that to miss out on our glorious moments of triumph is to miss out on life. That is because life is nothing more than a series of moments, each of which is filled with some experience or the other, with the experience in one moment adding up to the experience in the next moment, and to all the other succeeding moments, to create a life. That is why, when one misses the moments, one misses out on life. The time has come for me to celebrate my *glorious moments of triumph,* which I also call my *'I'* moments.

I completed my college degree.

I raised my four sons all alone.

I completed therapy to deal with childhood trauma.

I overcame normative conformity to eventually own my true and
authentic self.

I prioritize my self-care

I stepped out in faith to pursue my authentic destiny.

I completed my full term of office on the Fond du Lac City Council

I wrote and released a Gratitude Anthology.

I became the first published author in my family.

I bounced back from two divorces.

I learned to love myself.

I launched my first private community for empowering others to overcome trauma.

I continued to pursue my purpose, even after a tragic loss.

I forgave those who felt no remorse for hurting me.

By no means is this list exhaustive, I can assure you. In the final analysis, what we need to bear in mind is that, with self-celebration, there ought to be no special place, time, or even reason, behind our celebration. I consider my self-celebration simply for myself, and for myself alone. I encourage you to practice celebrating your successes as well. Celebrating yourself gives you a sense of confidence that says, *"I am unstoppable. I can accomplish whatever I set my heart upon."*

This is your reality. It is not unfounded bragging, although you do have bragging rights. Your reality is that you should enthusiastically step into the positive energy that comes along with acknowledging how you too have defied the odds. It is time to celebrate your successes. We celebrate our birthdays, anniversaries, and holidays. But, we hardly celebrate our accomplishments. That is unfortunate. Just as we mark the big events in our lives, we should also pay tribute to our accomplishments as well. On average, by the age of eighteen, we will have been praised and encouraged 30,000 times. In fact, we receive most of these by the time we are three years old. Somewhere along the way, we stop celebrating. Sadly, neglecting to celebrate your successes can cause you to slowly start to take a negative view of your own accomplishments. That is because, if you are not celebrating your accomplishments, you are focused on what you haven't yet accomplished instead of what you have already accomplished, and you are less likely to complete your goals. The good news is that celebrating your accomplishments can boost your confidence, and fuel your continued success.

Why it is So Important to Celebrate Your Successes

It is easy to celebrate the success of others. It is a natural human response to good news. Yet, we need to spare time to celebrate our own accomplishments too. It is important for us to celebrate our accomplishments because it actually feels good to do so. We like to feel good. Often, we are driven to make necessary changes in our lives, all so that we can feel *good, better, happier,* and *whole*. When something feels good, you are motivated to do more of it. If you want to be more successful, simply celebrate your successes. Additionally, the intentionality that comes from purposely acknowledging something that you did correctly places some focus on the positive, while minimizing what did not work. In my own case, I have the bad habit of being an overachiever, as I have mentioned previously in this book. The problem with being an overachiever is that you never sit long enough to reflect on your *win* because you are always thinking of the next goal. This is why it is important to intentionally celebrate every *win*, no matter how large, and no matter how small. This creates the success attitude that says, *"I have won before. I can win again!"*

I also developed the equally bad habit of being a *worry wart*, as a fallout of constant anxiety and panic over *lack*.

Thankfully, adulthood has compelled me to practice a totally different type of mindset than the one I was accustomed to. For instance, I now employ new techniques, such as declaring affirmations and regularly envisioning my success, to keep myself motivated to continue to aim for my goals. Focusing on the things I have already accomplished helps me to cultivate that vital space in my heart and mind that craves and nurtures even more and greater success. Affirming every day that I am a success and that I can succeed, builds up my own self-belief. Because I am aware of all the choices and hard work it took for me to accomplish all my goals, it seems only right that I take a moment to reflect, and to do so in a way that is memorable enough to ignite greater momentum for future successes. Taking a moment of pause, to notice and acknowledge your successes, is important because it causes you to view yourself as the success you long for, and so you attract more successes because you are once again practicing gratitude for what you have already accomplished.

Celebrating your successes allows you to develop a success mindset. When you position yourself as a winner, you open the door for more success. *Success begets success,* so it is only natural to build upon existing momentum, especially during events of celebration. In other words, your perception will become your reality. When you have arrived at an important milestone, instead of immediately moving on to the long list of things that you have to do next, spend some time reflecting on what you have accomplished and celebrating it. As you celebrate your wins, others look for ways to participate in what you have successfully built. The right partnerships are formed via a value-for-value exchange. This means that as you celebrate with others, there is a high probability they will be coming to the table with ways to expand upon what you have already achieved.

Celebrating your successes allows you to build on your confidence. Telling yourself that you can be successful and that you can accomplish things, will do wonders for your confidence. Instead of downplaying your achievements, attributing them to luck, or giving others the credit, it is important to acknowledge and celebrate them. Allow your accomplishments to become a reminder that you can succeed. After all, you have succeeded before.

Celebrating your successes will further motivate you. If you don't take the time to acknowledge your successes, it is easy to lose motivation. But, celebrating and acknowledging your victories, even if it is with a small reward, can help to keep you motivated. Conversely, if you fail to celebrate your accomplishments, you are training your brain to falsely believe that what you are doing isn't particularly exciting and important. If each day feels ordinary and unimportant, you will stop offering a hundred percent of yourself, and that can only produce mediocre results. Simply put, the lack of celebration will lead to a feeling of emptiness that will result in less focus and decreased performance over time.

When you celebrate your successes, you inspire others. When others join you in celebrating, they automatically partake in your happiness and are motivated to achieve their own goals as well. Your own celebration is contagious, and those around you want to share in your success, and as accomplishments are properly recounted, new ideas and opportunities are formed and shared. So, whether you go to the movies, out to dinner with friends, buy yourself something you've wanted for some time, or just take a day to do things that you enjoy, make sure that you find a way to celebrate. Simply celebrate what you want to see more of. Never forget to include others in your celebration. When celebrating success, it can be easy to forget others who may have helped us, in ways big or small, to reach the finish line. Including others in your celebration is a wonderful way to build and strengthen your connection with coworkers, loved ones, or others who helped you along the way. Give them specific feedback about the ways that they helped you achieve your goal and express gratitude for their help. People enjoy feeling helpful, appreciated, and connected. When you celebrate success with others, you are nurturing the kind of meaningful relationships that allow those same people to want to help you in the future.

How to Celebrate

There are so many ways in which you can celebrate, not only success but, *yourself*, as an individual. Believe it or not, you are worth celebrating. It took literally ages for me to develop the confidence to say that about myself. The truth is, I was afraid of my own abilities, perhaps because, at times, my accomplishments seemed unexplainable. The only explanation must be that God was at work with each accomplishment. *Defying the odds* has become just a part of who I am. What seemed impossible has always been made possible for me through God, resilience, perseverance, grit, and the sheer will to never give up, no matter how tough the battle seemed. I always believe that if God has performed miracles for me once, He certainly can accomplish even more such miracles.
I choose to celebrate myself every day, in some way, shape, form, or fashion. A celebration does not have to be elaborate to be meaningful. I like to measure the size of my celebration by the magnitude of what I'm celebrating. For instance, after concluding this chapter of this book tonight, I will celebrate by running a bubble bath, with lots of bubbles and bath bombs. I will wear pajamas that make me happy, after pampering myself with a body lotion that fills the entire room with a warm and

exhilarating fragrance. In this form of celebration, I totally engage myself in personal luxury by relaxing my mind and unwinding. Every now and again, I light candles to accompany my bubble bath and pour a glass of Risata Moscato D'Asti, a seductively sweet, fresh, and fragrant wine that boasts juicy stone fruit, tart citrus, and floral honey flavors. I might even garnish it with fresh strawberries and ice cubes to turn it into a cocktail. Then, I would switch on my echo dot and ask Alexa to play the Mary J. Blige station, and simply and languidly bask in the surreal ambiance of the moment.

At such times, I travel in my imagination to distant places. It is at such times that I titillate my own senses with words such as these:

The screen of my mind;
Filled with picturesque scenes from the beaches of the South Pacific.
The blue ocean;
Stretching as far as my eyes can see;
The waves;
Gargantuan and cascading;
One into the other;
Swirling in ever so majestic tides;
As they come crashing to the beach.
The oysters;
The pearls;
Glinting amongst millions of grains of sand.
The tropical palm trees;
Dotting the length of the beach;
For as far my eyes can glimpse.
The palm fronds;
Swaying gently to the rhythm of the tropical winds.

Doesn't that sound great? I can certainly tell you that it feels so good! This is how I celebrate *myself*. I do things that feel good and motivate me to do even better. If I was on a diet plan, I would celebrate by indulging myself in a *cheat day*, which meant chocolate, a rare treat for me. Each day, I celebrate myself by doing those little things that make me happy, like catching up on a Netflix series or finding ways to not be so serious. I would unleash my inner child by dancing, and singing at the top of my lungs. I have a special playlist that I created on my phone for emotions that run the gamut of *happy, sad, brokenhearted, joyful, feeling sexy,* or *loving.* This makes me happy because I love music so much. It is one of the biggest parts of my life, and it has the ability to help me transcend my current emotion, and take me to distant places in my imagination.

Yet, at times, I celebrate in big ways. I wait for my favorite artist to be in concert, and I get a front-row ticket to the show. I might take myself out to eat at my favorite places that serve the very best seafood, and sometimes, with friends and family that I know support me and love me. At other times, I celebrate *myself* by celebrating *others.* I took enormous pride in planning my sons' birthday parties since such events served to highlight just how hard I had worked to provide the celebration itself. I would always ask my sons what they wanted for their celebrations, and I would go above and beyond what they requested. As a single mom, this was a huge celebration for me, especially because my boys are so humble, and were always enormously appreciative of whatever I was able to provide. It truly doesn't take much to celebrate *you.* Simply become more intentional about celebrating *yourself,* because you are worth celebrating. If you were writing in the workbook that will eventually accompany this book, this is where I would ask you to list all the ways in which you could celebrate *yourself*.

Reinvent Yourself Through Prayer and Meditation

My story, through which you have accompanied me on the pages of this book, has been filled with despair and pain. Because of heartbreak, abandonment, and betrayal, I have cried rivers of tears. I have lost friends. Family members have passed away, leaving huge voids in my life. My dreams have been shattered, often by those whom I loved and trusted. My finances have been precarious, hardly ever constantly flowing. Yet, I have hope. I have confidence, not in myself, but in God. He has never failed me. Because God has *had my back* all these years, I am always looking forward to what happens next after the devastation. I dare not claim that it has been my own power working to help me *defy the odds* all these years. That would be an unforgivable lie. It has been the *Power of God* at work in my life. God has sustained me, strengthened me, held me, and encouraged me. God has given me the strength it takes to begin again after a disaster, a setback, a letdown, or a disappointment. God has sufficiently fortified me to try new endeavors, change my plans, relocate, and begin again as a new person, and a much more confident *Arletta*. At those times when I felt lost, and in which even others deemed me lost, not necessarily physically, but emotionally, mentally, and spiritually, I have maintained my confidence by knowing that God always knows where I am.

You cannot successfully reinvent yourself without a solid relationship with God. God is the only one who knows exactly who you are, where you are, and who He has purposed you to be. Therefore, I have created a life that is founded upon constant communication with God, so that I can continue to proceed in the direction that pleases God, rather than the direction that my flesh is pulling me towards. My prayer time with God quietens my spirit and helps me to see things more clearly. For instance, not too long ago, I received an eviction notice for defaulting on my rent. Naturally, I was shaken up a bit. I have been homeless before. I have had moments in which I had not even a dollar to my name. Yet, God sustained me. Because I have built a life that is heavily reliant on prayer, and which trusts God to handle the cares of this world for me, I trusted God to step in on my behalf. As it happened, I was chasing my dreams, believing that I was right where God was directing me to, but it seemed that every opportunity that came my way for sustainable livelihood would somehow fall through. Seemingly, it was pure devastation.

Finally, I found that it was more important for me to look *inwards*, rather than *outwards*. I trusted God. He made a way out of no way, and all my debts are settled in heaven and on Earth. God is my provider. Those who employ me are mere vessels used by God to supply my needs. Those who hire me to fulfill their event needs are instruments used by God for me to fulfill my purpose of helping others to make the transition from *trauma to triumph.* Having a life of prayer and meditation promotes newness and purposeful living. This has been the key to my every success, even in the process of writing this book. Only God could have made this work possible. I believe it never would have manifested had I not petitioned God for the desire to become the first published author in my family. Now, look at what you hold in your hands. It is the manifestation of a life that has been yielded to God's will and purpose. I believe that without God in the picture, I am nothing. Without God, I would surely fail. This story is not mine. It is God's own story. I am merely a messenger. Turn the page to read my farewell note to you. On that note, you will learn that it was my predestination to not only *live* a legacy, but to *leave* one.

A Farewell Note to You
Wearing a New Mask

---

*"Perhaps the butterfly is proof that you can go through a great
deal of darkness yet become something beautiful."*

- Unknown

Dear Co-Traveler on The Journey *From Trauma To Triumph,*

If you are reading these words, it means you have taken the
trouble to journey with me through the pages of this book. I
thank you for that. Accept my sincere gratitude for making my
effort a worthwhile one. The road of life can be long, hard and
arduous. It is harder still if there is no hand to hold as you
trudge along, weary from the burden of it all. The effort of
writing this book itself was a journey all by itself. In reading
this book to the end, you were merely accompanying me on the
journey. Thank you for holding my hand, even as I held your
hand, as we made the journey together.

The toughest part of overcoming trauma is forgiving
yourself. If there is one final message I would like you to take
from our joint journey, it is that we must forgive ourselves, and
dare to set those vital boundaries that will eventually protect
who we are becoming. Each and every day, we must meet the
challenge of being better than we were yesterday. People will
always be quick to judge you, especially when they don't know
your story. That is why, anytime I remember all the times I
have failed, and then gotten back on my feet, I am humbled by
the grace of God upon my life.

As we part ways, I ask you to reflect on my *trauma* and:

Remember that I endured unthinkable trauma and abuse at the hands of my father.

Remember that my family suffered, in lack and in poverty. Yet, my mother found many ways to create a meal out of nothing.

Remember that I endured two emotionally, mentally, verbally, and physically abusive marriages.

Remember that I was a high school dropout.

Remember that I became a prostitute at the age of 15.

Remember that I became a single mother at the age of 16

Remember that I dropped out of school to hold down two jobs to take care of my son.

Remember that I spent 75% of my life seeking validation from others.

Remember that I suffered through the chills of normative conformity in hopes of finding a sense of belonging

Remember that I lost myself pretending to be what I believed everyone else needed.

Remember that I suffered abandonment, betrayal, and rejection mostly from those who God entrusted to love me.

Remember that I started college, but quit three times.

Then, I ask you to celebrate my *triumph* with me as you:

Remember that I was the first college graduate in my family.

Remember that I graduated with a Bachelor of Communication and Business Minor with honors and distinction.

Remember that I did an associate's Degree in Leadership Development, along with four additional certifications.

Remember that I am the first person in my family to own a home.

Remember that I am the first black woman to work in a financial institution in the city of Fond du lac, Wisconsin.

Remember that I founded a nonprofit, "Peculiar Princess Project, Inc." to create a sense of belonging for little girls just like me.

Remember that I was the first person of color in the history of that community to serve on its City Council.

Remember that I was the first black woman to own and operate her own restaurant in the same city.

Remember that I am the first nationally-recognized award winner from the National Community Action Partnerships in the State of Wisconsin.

Remember that I discovered that my story is powerful and I now live to speak and speak to live!

Remember that I discovered my passion and purpose in leading others to their transformation from the stage.

Remember that I finally learned to celebrate myself, authentically!

Remember that I now guide individuals on their journey to transition from trauma to triumph as a trauma recovery coach.

As I write the closing words of this book, I can only give God the glory and honor for allowing me to be a traveler on such a remarkable journey. I believe that I have successfully redefined the generational baton handed to me, and as I share my story with you, my sincere hope is that my story of courage, perseverance, and resilience will be of immense and everlasting benefit to you. I thank you, most sincerely, for keeping faith with me to read up to the final words of this book. As I take my leave of you, I invite you to tap into your soul's deepest desires, and should you find yourself short of your own expectations, set goals to achieve those ideals, and start to act to reinforce those goals. Discover exactly what it is that you want from life, and act in accordance with the values and goals you have set for yourself. Yes, simply decide to continue to be the best version of yourself for the rest of your life. Indeed, my humble verdict is that I have *defied the odds*, and that is my sincere wish for you too. Please accept the assurance of my love and affection always.

Arletta Allen
Arlington, Texas
United States of America
November 2022

About the Author
Arletta Allen

Arletta Allen is the CEO of Authentically Arletta Unlimited LLC. Arletta is a best-selling author, dynamic professional speaker, and trauma recovery coach. Arletta graduated with distinction from Marian University of Fond du lac, Wisconsin. She is recognized as Marian University's 2019 Communications Student of the Year and is known as an academic scholar holding a Bachelor of Communication (BOC), Leadership Development Business degree, and certifications in Organizational Management, Healthcare Leadership, Principles of Leadership, and Human Resource Development. Arletta is a contributing best-selling author of the gratitude anthology, "WhoO Influenced You? Three Relationships that Transformed my Life" along with Dr. George C. Fraser and MBN owner Mr. Stan Matthews. She has also authored "Defying the Odds: "Making the Transition from Trauma to Triumph" as well as the forthcoming 90-day journal titled, " Baby Let Me Tell You: A Mother's Wisdom for Everyday Living".

Arletta is dedicated to leading as many as possible on the journey to overcome insurmountable odds in their professional and personal development. She has worked with many reputable organizations and earned her position as an expert in leadership, resilience, and authenticity. Arletta's clients describe her as powerful, funny, relatable, authentic, transparent, and vulnerable. Arletta is prompt, timely, easy to work with, and communicates well. Audiences love her practical strategies they can apply personally and professionally. She delivers with passion, guiding her audience to effectively strengthen and elevate their leadership vision to new heights. Arletta has a relatable humor that compels audiences to laugh while they are being empowered.

Arletta engages her audience from the moment she steps in front of them and leaves them with empowering tools and focused mindsets that they will use long after she is gone. She is nationally recognized through national community action partnerships of America the Sargent Shriver Award for self-sufficiency. She was awarded the Wisconsin State Community Action Award for Self-Sufficiency. Featured as the cover story in Inspire Magazine, The first person of color in history to serve on the city council in Fond du Lac, Wisconsin, and also receive the key to the city. Arletta was selected out of hundreds of applicants to deliver a TEDx talk on Authenticity.

Arletta has 14 plus years of experience working within financial institutions. She has been retained to facilitate and deliver keynote presentations at Colleges, Universities, Community Action Partnerships, Jeremy Anderson, Dr. Cheryl Woods, Ashley Kirkwood, UBMS (Upward Bound Math & Science), TRIO Programs, Technical Colleges, TEDx, Ebony Vision, as a Local Government Elected Official, SHRM Chapters (Society for Human Resource Management), Domestic Violence Shelters, FDL Area Women's Fund, Color Brave Initiatives, Diversity, Equity, & Inclusion Keynote, UW Extension, Entrepreneurial Bootcamps, Ripon College Panelist,

Commencement Speaker Moraine Park Technical College. She is a highly sought-after and frequent guest of the media on the topics of leadership, authenticity, resilience, and defying the odds. Arletta regularly contributes her expertise to many podcast interviews In Our Words Podcast, Infamous Mothers Podcast, and FDL Area Women's Fund. Inspire Magazine, NBC, NBC Nightly News, Fox Valley 365 Magazine, New North Magazine and so much more.